CARING
FOR A
PARENT IN
LATER LIFE

'08,

CARING FOR A PARENT IN LATER LIFE

JUDITH CAMERON

AUTHOR

Judith Cameron is a journalist and writer with extensive personal experience of caring. She is a regular contributor to *The Guardian* and other publications on aspects of care, where her work o′
and family issues. H

LifeGuides are comr.
207–221 Pentonville Road, London N1 9UZ and can be purchased via www.helptheaged.org.uk or from bookshops

For a full list of Help the Aged publications, see the website, telephone 020 7239 1946 or email publications@helptheaged.org.uk.

First published 2008

Trade distribution by Turnaround Publisher Services Ltd

British Library Cataloguing in Publication Data
A catalogue record for this book is available from the British Library

ISBN 978-1-84598-027-6

Designed and typeset by Price Watkins Design
Printed and bound in England by CPI Mackay Ltd

CONTENTS

CONTENTS, continued

1

YOU AND YOUR PARENTS

YOU AND YOUR PARENTS

'With both of my parents in their late 80s and my father registered blind, I am just waiting for a crisis and dreading what it will be.' *(daughter)*

'Mum gets upset that she can't just hop on the bus and come over like she used to. I don't mind driving over to collect her, but she hates the idea of relying on someone else. She's always been so independent.' *(son)*

'The way she talks to me sometimes, you'd think I'd had my brain replaced, not my hip.' *(father)*

For most of us, our parents were the first people with whom we built a long and enduring relationship. As a child, we relied on them to look after us, and even as we grew into independent adults we valued their help and advice in coping with the daily demands our work and relationships made upon us. Parents could often be relied upon to help with decorating and gardening, or perhaps to give us a break from the children and have them to stay for weekends or holidays. For our children when they were small, grandparents could be a wealth of stories from the 'olden days'; they had time to sit and talk when we always seemed to be busy. As they grew through the pain of adolescence, grandparents may have offered sensible but unconditional love when we, their parents, were less understanding.

However, as we grow older we become aware that our parents are ageing, perhaps very noticeably. Gradually, instead of us needing their help and support, the relationship goes into reverse. It can be quite a scary feeling to discover that your previously strong and healthy father would now struggle to mow the lawn or put up a curtain pole. And your mother, whom you might have thought of as being so capable, is becoming increasingly forgetful.

Of course, your father probably finds it scary too. He may be unwilling to accept his diminishing strength and insist on doing things that subsequently exhaust him and make him ill for a few days. He may make excuses for your mother's forgetfulness while she insists on continuing to invite the whole extended family for Sunday lunch and subsequently becomes upset and flustered when it turns out to be rather too much for her. Meanwhile, we may be noticing that our parents' home is not being kept as clean as it used to be, and we may have other concerns about how they are coping with life.

WHAT CAN YOU DO? HOW CAN YOU HELP?

One thing you must not do, no matter how difficult or strange your parent's behaviour may have become, is to treat him or her like a child.

In the same way that those of us who are parents recognise that whatever happens, our children will always remain our children, we too will always remain our parents' children. It can be difficult to take the upper hand with regard to a parent's behaviour and well-being; until now, it has always been us who have sought their approval and support. Even if you have not grown up in a supportive and affectionate family, you may still feel daunted by the prospect of parents who are no longer able to look after themselves.

On the other hand, it is probable that your parents will have mixed emotions too. Even if they have started to recognise that their reflexes are slower than before, that they have to write everything down if they are to remember it and that it has become difficult to get in and out of the bath, they will not want to be a burden on you. Nor will they want to feel useless.

This is perhaps the time to sit down and consider the future. One possibility is that the time may not be far away when someone else may need to look after their property and financial affairs, and possibly to make decisions about their health and personal welfare. It is now, while your parent is still relatively fit and mentally acute, that you should discuss what they want to happen in the event of their health deteriorating. Talk to your parents and discuss the merit of arranging a lasting power of attorney (see page 121). It may never be needed, but if it is, it will make it much easier for you to provide support.

LIFE-CHANGING EVENTS

Bereavement Perhaps, following an active life through their 50s and 60s and a long and happy marriage, one of your parents dies. Along with coping with your own grief, you may be coming to terms with the fact that you will have to support your remaining parent more than you ever have before.

Loss of memory We are all capable of forgetting someone's birthday, or where we left our keys, but you may have noticed that your parent has become more forgetful than usual or forgetful in a way that you find strange; perhaps they cannot remember whether or not they have eaten their lunch or supper.

Illness Your parent may have had a stroke or heart attack or suffered significant deterioration in sight or hearing that has made you aware that it is now much more difficult for them to live independently. Arthritis, a common problem among older people, may be affecting your parent's ability to cope with household chores and shopping. Dementia is another debilitating condition that can seriously affect your parent's ability to live independently.

Falls These represent the most frequent and serious type of accident in the over-65s, with one older person dying every five hours as a result of a fall in the home. Falls often result in a hospital stay. If your parent has been in hospital following a fall, perhaps you are starting to wonder how they will manage when they get home.

General decline in health and fitness Maybe you have noticed that your parents' general health is declining, and that they tire easily and have become reluctant to go out with friends or continue with hobbies. Perhaps they appear less confident about driving or going anywhere on their own.

The list of warning signs (see box on page 11) suggests the sorts of situation that may present themselves and make you aware that your relationship with your parent will need to change.

> *Whatever the trigger that signals a change in your relationship, try very hard to allow your parent to retain their status, their dignity and their place in the family.*

Even if your mother is no longer able to cook as she once did, she will still be able to let you know her secret for a perfect Victoria sponge, or the best way to get ink stains out of a shirt. Even if you know her tips, ask for them again, and make her feel valued. In the same way, your father's method of keeping slugs off the runner beans will be as efficient as it ever was. Let your parents know that you value their advice and expertise, and that they still have an important role in your life.

Involve your parents in decisions about your own life: maybe ask their opinion about problems you may be having at work, or with your children. Even if they are forgetful or less able physically, it does not mean that their experiences of life are less valid than they used to be. Your parents need to be actively involved and included.

WHAT IS CARING?

'I'm not that worried about the future at the moment because Mum's managing so well on her own. Sooner or later, we'll have to talk about what she'll want later on but I'm not in a hurry.' *(son)*

'Now that Dad's not there and with us living so far away, I do wonder what Mum's neighbours think of me as a daughter. But I'm on my own and the children are still young: what can I do?' *(daughter)*

'My family could recognise that I am getting older and that I perhaps could be considered to require consideration from time to time. "Help" seems one-way traffic in the opposite direction.' (*mother*)

Caring can take different guises and include so many tasks that it can often be difficult to define. Maybe your frail parent lives nearby and you drop in daily, perhaps taking a meal, or you go shopping with them once a week and organise their doctor's appointments. Despite working full-time in an office and looking after your own household, you are still their carer if you are the main person who is looking after their well-being. If you live far away from your parent, you probably phone regularly, check that bills are paid and arrange for someone to come in and help with the housework: hence, you are still your parent's carer.

WHEN SHOULD YOU GET INVOLVED?

It may be when you become aware that your father is no longer as strong or competent as he was before a minor accident or illness. Alternatively, you may have recently suffered the loss of a much-loved mother and, as well as coping with your own grief, have realised that your father is not managing to look after himself as well as he did before – possibly because he had previously relied heavily on his wife to care for him. You may have noticed that he is not as particular with his personal care and dresses sloppily, or has become increasingly forgetful. Maybe you have started to worry that your mother is losing weight and that she is not eating properly.

HOW SHOULD YOU GET INVOLVED?

This will depend greatly on the relationship that you have with your parent, where you live and whether you have a family that depends on you financially or emotionally. It is important to consider seriously how much responsibility for your parent you can reasonably manage. Do you have siblings who live close by? It is good to be able to share the care and worry that will probably develop as your parent becomes older, increasingly frail and needy.

Initially, you will need to talk to your parent about your concerns and discover whether they too are aware of their diminished health and well-being. If they have always lived independently and in their own home, it is unlikely that it will immediately be appropriate for them to move elsewhere, or for their lifestyle to change dramatically unless they have suffered a serious illness. At the same time, if they have recently been bereaved and are not used to living alone, loneliness and possibly isolation may become issues for which they are ill-prepared.

Ask your parent if they would mind if you contacted their doctor and any other health professionals they see, to make sure that they have your details should there ever be a serious cause for concern with your parent's health. In addition, if you do not already know their neighbours, it would be a good idea to introduce yourself and ask for their telephone numbers in case of emergency.

Despite making yourself more easily available to your parent in case of need, you should also encourage them to maintain their independence. It is easy to offer someone you love more help than they need, but for your parent to retain their dignity and self-esteem they should be supported in their own efforts rather than pampered. At the same time, make sure they know that you want them to manage their own affairs so that they remain self-sufficient, not because you do not want to help. As in all relationships, good communication is vital for success.

This may be the beginning of a very long period during which your parent or parents will need increasing support. Although there may be times you will enjoy, of great happiness and pleasure, there will almost certainly be times when you become impatient and frustrated with your parent. They may not recognise that they need reminding of appointments or the need to do their laundry, and even if they do they may feel resentful that they are no longer as capable as they once were. This may make them difficult and argumentative, which in turn will make you more annoyed. Subsequently, you may feel guilty for being angry. Such feelings, on both sides, are completely normal, and knowing this will help you to deal with your own. Caring for your parent will not always be plain sailing. Consequently, you need to make sure that you are aware of all the help your parent is entitled to have, and of anything that might be available to support you, too.

KEEPING RECORDS

One advantage of looking after someone as they become older and frailer is that, barring illness or accident, you will have time to plan ahead and be organised. To this end, at the beginning of the caring period it is a good idea to get a notebook and file that will only be used in connection with your parent.

In the notebook you can make a list of all relevant names, telephone numbers and addresses of friends, neighbours, health and care professionals and other useful services. When you have a conversation with any professional, it is worth keeping a record of what was said and when.

As your parent becomes increasingly dependent on others, this notebook could prove invaluable. Your parent (and you) will have increasing contact with various departments of the NHS and the local authority and, despite good intentions, you will discover that one support department or organisation may have little or no contact with another. If you can keep a record of dates and of conversations, it will help the whole social support system for your parent run more smoothly.

HEALTH PROFESSIONALS

Doctor (GP) If you have concerns about your parent's general well-being, the first port of call should be to your parent's GP surgery. This may be a group practice, but your parent will be registered with a specific doctor and this is whom you should try to contact. The doctor will not only give your parent general medical advice but is also the point of referral to other medical services and specialists. Unless your parent has given specific instructions, their doctor will not be allowed to discuss their medical needs with you. So it is important, early on, to make sure that your parent is happy for you to be able to talk to their doctor about any problems.

It may be a good idea to discuss the possibility of arranging a lasting power of attorney to ensure that if at any future time your parent is not in a position to give permission, you will be able to make decisions on their behalf. This is a very important issue if your parent has been diagnosed with a condition that will worsen over time, such as Alzheimer's or Parkinson's disease.

Your parent's doctor and surgery staff, who are likely to deal with a good many older people, should be a great source of information and advice.

District nurse If your parent has ongoing nursing needs at home – for example, to have dressings changed daily, following a fall – a district nurse will usually visit. The nurse can also give advice and training in basic medical skills if you want to do these yourself. If you are concerned about your parent's medical needs and the doctor has not suggested a visit by the district nurse, ask for one and a medical care assessment will be made.

Health visitor A health visitor is a trained nurse who will appraise the health requirements of someone who needs care in the home. Sometimes, the district nurse will make the appraisal and subsequently make contact with other health professionals as deemed necessary. The health visitor or district nurse will give general advice on diet, exercise, skin care and incontinence. If necessary, a referral will be made to a specialist. For more information on incontinence, see chapter 4, on Health and Well-being.

Community psychiatric nurse If your parent is diagnosed with a mental health problem, the community psychiatric nurse will visit. She can give advice, monitor medication and provide treatment.

Speech therapist If your parent has suffered a stroke, their speech and swallow may have been affected. They will have already have been assessed by a speech therapist before leaving hospital and will consequently have follow-up appointments, probably at the local hospital or GP surgery.

Occupational therapist If your parent's home needs adaptations or specific equipment is needed to help them cope with life, an occupational therapist will advise on what is required. An occupational therapist is frequently involved in a person's Community Care Assessment (see 'Care assessment', below).

Other health professionals Your parent can be referred to many other professionals through their doctor's surgery. These include **chiropodists** or **podiatrists** for feet, **orthopists** for specialist footwear and splints, **dentists** for teeth, **opticians** for eyes, **dieticians** for advice on eating. Possibilities for advice on cancer care include the **Cancerbackup** helpline or the **Macmillan CancerLine** (see chapter 6 for both).

SOCIAL SERVICES PROFESSIONALS

Social worker Each local authority has a social services department which is responsible for the care of vulnerable members of its community. Within social services there are usually specialist teams for different sections of the community – for example, mental health, childcare or older people. The team members are usually called social workers or sometimes case workers. If you are concerned about how your parent is managing at home, you can ask for a Community Care Assessment (see below) by a social worker. It is the social worker's job to ensure that your parent is able to access whatever help is deemed appropriate and to be the point of contact between your parent and the local authority's services, such as day care centres, meals on wheels or home care assistants. The social worker will also be involved in the assessment of what, if any, financial benefits your parent is entitled to.

Home care provider If your parent is assessed as needing help in the home, maybe with washing and dressing, shopping, preparing food, laundry and cleaning, it is the duty of the local authority to make it available. Previously, 'home helps' were employees of the local authority and worked within their boundaries. Nowadays, most home care is provided by private care agencies that are under contract to the local authority.

CARE ASSESSMENT

'I didn't know what it was called, but it was useful to be able to sit down with someone and work out what Dad wanted. The woman was very nice.' (*daughter*)

If your parent has been ill, in hospital or simply becomes less able to look after themselves, it may be time to consider a Care Assessment, to ascertain what services are needed to make their life easier. The assessment, carried out by the social services (or social work) department of your parent's local council, will take a broad look at your parent's present situation, their health, their mobility, their home and their needs. Each local council has its own rules, often called 'eligibility criteria', that define for whom it will provide services. Your parent's 'assessed needs' are those needs that fall within their local council's eligibility criteria.

Unfortunately, this means that they may not be offered all the services you think they need. However, once the local council has assessed your parent as having met its criteria, it must then provide services to meet those 'assessed needs' – it cannot just say it has run out of money.

In essence, the community care assessment enables social services to find out what a person's care needs are and to decide which services could help to meet these needs. The social services department will work closely with other services, such as health services and voluntary organisations, when assessing a person's needs.

It is worth remembering that a local authority will not arrange services unless a community care assessment (sometimes called a needs assessment) has taken place (see box).

COMMUNITY CARE OR NEEDS ASSESSMENT

This is likely to involve:

- talking to the person concerned and their carer, where appropriate, to find out what their needs and views are
- assessing the person's health and disabilities and considering what they can and cannot do
- considering the person's present living arrangements and arrangements for care.

If your parent is willing, it is a good idea if you too can be present for the assessment. It can be difficult for a proud and independent older person to admit how difficult certain tasks have become: if you are there, you can offer moral support as well as offering gentle reminders about problems. The person who makes the assessment should look at the emotional and social side of your parent's life as well as any physical difficulties they might have. They should take into account any health or housing needs your parent may have; and contact any other health and social care professionals who need to be involved in the assessment and care.

Your parent may need a specialist assessment for a particular need (such as adaptations to their home), or a more comprehensive assessment of the different sorts of help they need to stay in their home. This assessment might include several people such as a social worker, occupational therapist, nurse, and possibly even a housing officer if they have special housing needs.

WAITING FOR AN ASSESSMENT

Your parent may have to wait for a while for an assessment, depending on how urgently the local authority thinks they need help. For example, if they need a grab rail for their bathroom they may have to wait a few weeks. But if they need somebody to help them get out of bed in the mornings they should be assessed as a priority case.

There is no set time-frame within which you can insist on your parent having an assessment, but if you feel that the waiting time is unreasonable you should put in a complaint (see next section).

BEING INVOLVED IN THE ASSESSMENT

As their child and someone who cares for them, it can be very helpful for you to be involved in the assessment. However, social services should not assume that you will automatically be able to carry out caring duties. Nevertheless, what you are able and willing to do must be considered when your parent's needs are being assessed. If your duties are onerous, you can ask to have a separate assessment (a carer's assessment) of your needs as well as finding out what respite services are available to give you a break. See the section 'Support for carers', page 28.

WHAT HAPPENS AT THE ASSESSMENT

Somebody should visit your parent personally. The assessment should not be done over the phone or by letter. Your parent's needs cannot be properly assessed in that way. If your parent does not receive a visit you can put in a complaint that their needs have not been properly assessed.

The assessment is about your parent and their needs. They should be involved and their wishes should be taken into account. So it is helpful if you can help your parent think in advance about what they want to tell the person who is doing the assessment (see box).

BEFORE THE ASSESSMENT

- If you have agreed to be there, make sure the appointment is convenient for you as well as your parent.
- Suggest your parent keep a diary for a couple of days beforehand, noting details of all the times during the day and night when they need help.
- Remind your parent to think about bad days as well as good. Although it is good to have a positive outlook they need to be realistic about what help is required.
- Do not assume that the person doing the assessment knows what type of help will be required. This will probably be the first time they have met your parent and all they will know is what you and your parent tell them. Give them as much detail as you can, even if you think it is not important.
- You may find it useful to draw up a checklist with your parent of the activities with which they have difficulties; and the services and equipment you feel might help them to cope at home.
- If your parent has difficulty communicating or if English is not their first language and you cannot adequately speak on their behalf, social services should make special arrangements so that your parent can play a full part in their assessment.

AFTER THE ASSESSMENT

Your parent should be given a written copy of the assessment. They may be asked to sign it. If so, make sure that they and you have read it carefully before agreeing to sign. If there is anything you or your parent do not agree with, add a note. Be aware that your parent is also entitled to refuse to sign it.

Once your parent's needs have been assessed a care plan should be provided, detailing what services will be provided and who will provide them. Your parent should be given the name of the person who will be responsible for their care services. The person may be a social worker and may be called a care manager. This person should check regularly that the services are right for your parent and that the assessed needs have not changed. Your parent's local council can:

- directly provide its own services;
- arrange for services to be provided by voluntary organisations and private agencies; or
- give your parent cash, known as Direct Payments, to arrange and manage their own care (see 'Care in your parent's home', page 55).

Your parent can request a re-assessment of needs at any time if they feel that the package of care is no longer meeting their needs. This is not unusual, and if you feel your parent is becoming less able you should encourage them to contact social services or, if necessary, make contact yourself.

MAKING A COMPLAINT

LOCAL AUTHORITY COMPLAINTS

You can use the complaints procedure of your parent's local authority if:

- your parent has been refused an assessment or re-assessment of their needs;
- you feel that your parent is being asked to wait an unreasonable length of time to have their needs assessed;
- you do not feel the assessment took into account all of your parent's needs;
- you feel that the services your parent is receiving are not meeting their needs;
- your parent is being asked to wait a long time for equipment or adaptations; or
- you feel your parent's charges for care are unreasonable.

The local authority should provide you with a leaflet about its complaints procedure and have a complaints officer who can advise you.

There are usually three stages to the complaints procedure:

- informal stage
- formal stage, involving a letter to the named complaints officer or Director of Social Services (or Director of Social Work in Scotland)
- review stage – an independent review of the complaint.

If you are not satisfied with the result from this you can complain to the local authority ombudsman.

You can also contact your parent's local councillor or MP. If it is an issue that is affecting many people in the area the local press may be interested. An alternative to the complaints procedure is to contact the monitoring officer at your parent's council. This person is responsible for making sure that the authority is carrying out all its legal obligations.

NHS COMPLAINTS

You can use the NHS complaints procedure if:

- you have a complaint about the services your parent receives from the NHS; or
- the NHS is not providing services or equipment to meet their needs.

You usually have to make a complaint within six months of becoming aware that there is a problem.

Each NHS service should have a leaflet explaining its complaints procedure – ask for a copy. It should also have a member of staff who is responsible for complaints and can explain how the system works.

There are usually two stages to the NHS complaints procedure:

- **local resolution** This involves putting in a complaint to the individual NHS service that you are unhappy with (for example, your parent's GP surgery, district nurse service, chiropody service, hospital or any other NHS service)

■ **independent review** You should be told how to ask for an independent review when you receive the letter telling you the outcome of your complaint.

If you have gone through the NHS complaints procedure but are not satisfied with the way your complaint has been handled, you can complain to the health service ombudsman.

FURTHER ADVICE ON MAKING A COMPLAINT
For further advice on how to make a complaint about your parent's local authority or the NHS:
- ■ call SeniorLine, a free advice line run by Help the Aged (see chapter 6)
- ■ contact your local Citizens Advice Bureau or Age Concern: either may be able to help you to make a complaint.

BEING A CARER

'I'm only doing for my mother what I know she'd do for me.' (*daughter*)

'We are still able to help our children out with babysitting and school collections, but should we need help in the future, we are confident it would be there.' (*parents*)

'Now that he's alone, my sister and I both phone him daily to check he's all right and have a chat.' (*son*)

It is estimated that every year 2 million people become carers and many of these will be looking after one or both of their parents, so remember that you are not alone. Becoming a carer can be bewildering, confusing and frightening. No one is superhuman and all carers need some support and back-up.

Various organisations are able to give advice: Help the Aged, Carers UK and the local Citizens Advice Bureau, among others (see chapter 6 for sources of information). and below is a list from Carers UK of things to do for yourself when it has become apparent that you are going to become more responsible for a parent's care.

■ **Accept that you are a carer**

Recognising yourself as a carer is the very first step to getting the support you need. Many of us do not see ourselves as carers straight away: we are just the grown-up son or daughter of our parents. We are simply doing what anyone would, caring unpaid for a loved one, helping them through when they are unable to do things for themselves. The fact is that you are also a carer, and there are things that you need to know. No one likes to be labelled, but recognising yourself as a carer can be the gateway to getting a range of help and support.

■ **Include your family and friends**

Many carers of parents turn to other family members and friends for support, and to help them to take a break from caring. It is important that you do not insist on trying to cope alone, as this can impact on your own health. Speak to the rest of your family and your friends and make sure they know the extent of your caring role. Many family members or friends may not realise the level of care you are providing; or they may be embarrassed, or afraid that you might think they are interfering. Other people may be reluctant to ask if you need help in case you get the wrong end of the stick and think they are saying you cannot cope. Sadly, some people do not know how to react to illness, dementia or disability and they find it awkward, so the onus might be on you to make the moves.

■ **Tell your GP**

Although there is no national register for carers, make sure that you tell your GP that you are now caring for your parent, and ask the doctor to write the details on your notes. If your GP surgery has got its act together it will ensure that, as a carer, you receive a regular health check and, if necessary, a flu jab. If they know you are a carer, some

GPs offer special flexibility with appointments, or are more willing to make home visits. Carers are usually busy and may find it difficult to make time for their own health care. A good GP who understands carers should be able to help you get all kinds of help, such as counselling, other medical services, and referrals to your local social services.

■ **Tell social services**

Social services, which are part of your local authority, provide a range of services to carers and people with disabilities. In Scotland they are called Social Work Departments and in Northern Ireland Health and Social Services Trusts. They should be one of your first contacts, as it is important they know that you are looking after your parent. As a carer, you are entitled to a carer's assessment, which looks at your needs and how you, as a carer, can be supported. Social services can provide replacement care to give you a break, help with aids and adaptations to make life easier or simply be a back-up in an emergency. You can call your local social services directly and speak to them about your role as a carer. Alternatively, your GP can refer you. Even if you choose not to have a carer's assessment, it is advisable to let social services know that you are a carer, should a time arise when you need urgent assistance.

■ **Tell people at work**

As a working carer, you are likely to need a range of support at different times – from access to a telephone to check on your parent's well-being, to leave arrangements that work around hospital discharge. Telling work you are a carer is not always an easy step and you might feel it depends on whether your employer is likely to be supportive. Find out, by asking your colleagues, personnel officer or union representative. There may be existing support that you are not aware of, or you may find that your employer is open to exploring ways to support carers. Colleagues can be very supportive, and it may help simply to discuss your situation with someone you can trust at work. You might even find that other colleagues are also carers, and that together you are more able to talk to your employer about ways in which you could be supported. Carers UK has information for employers on how supporting carers can benefit their business. This can help with your case.

■ Claim your entitlements

The benefit system is complex, and many people who are new to caring are unsure what they should be claiming. Many people are put off claiming by means-testing or complicated forms, but remember that the benefits system is there to help and you are entitled to claim. A number of benefits are available to carers, and it is important to ensure that you have the relevant information. Benefits can also act as a gateway to other help, such as Council Tax rebates (now referred to as Council Tax Benefit) or help with prescriptions.

■ Find your nearest carers' group or centre

Carers' groups, carers' centres and branches of Carers UK all give support to carers by providing information, arranging social events and giving carers time to speak to other carers about problems or experiences. Many carers find carers' groups a great source of support.

■ Take care of yourself

It is easy to neglect yourself when you are busy caring for someone. However, as a carer it is important that you look after yourself. At the very least, you will not be much use to your parent if you make yourself ill through caring. Sadly, one in five carers report that their health suffers as a direct result of caring. For example, without proper training carers are especially prone to back problems. Many of the most serious health problems carers suffer from, such as heart disease or mental breakdown, are a direct result of stress. Caring without a break, without proper sleep and without support is extremely stressful. It is crucial that you recognise this and take it seriously. Remember that a little can go a long way so, when you can, try to take some time out to do something for yourself: read a magazine, visit a friend, watch a TV programme or go for a walk.

■ Think about the future

As hard as it might be to contemplate, there will come a time when you are no longer caring. When caring ends it can be extremely hard. By facing the future and thinking about life after caring you can minimise the shock when the time comes. Many people say that when caring ends they feel cast adrift, without purpose or direction. Although caring can be all-consuming, it is important that you keep as much of your own life going as you can – work, friends, hobbies and interests.

SUPPORT FOR CARERS

Do not immediately dismiss the idea of having a Carer's Assessment from social services. The kind of help and support you can get as a carer includes:
■ respite care to give you a break;
■ emotional support from other carers;
■ help with caring; and
■ help with household tasks and activities for the person you care for.

Before you have an assessment you might want to think about the following:
■ are you getting enough sleep?
■ are you able to get out and do things by yourself?
■ do you feel that your health is being affected by caring?
■ are you able to cope with other family commitments?
■ are you finding juggling work and caring difficult?

Talk to the person doing your assessment about these and any other issues that you think may affect your ability to continue caring.

CARER'S ALLOWANCE

'I've never bothered claiming because I still do work sporadically and it's just too complicated.' (*daughter*)

Carer's Allowance is the main benefit for carers. The pitifully low basic rate of £50.55 a week will apply in 2008–9.

You can get Carer's Allowance for looking after your parent if:

- you look after your parent for at least 35 hours each week, and
- your parent gets Attendance Allowance or the middle or higher rate of the care component of Disability Living Allowance (refer to the section on Disability Benefits), and
- you are aged 16 or over, and
- you are not studying for more than 21 hours a week, and
- you do not earn more than £87 a week (2007–8 limit) from work (after some deductions), and
- you satisfy UK residence and immigration rules

NB If you are getting State Retirement Pension, Incapacity Benefit, Bereavement Benefit or any other 'earnings replacement' benefit of more than the rate of Carer's Allowance, you cannot be paid Carer's Allowance.

If this is the case, you could have 'underlying entitlement' to Carer's Allowance, which can help you to get more money from other benefits (e.g. an extra amount of Income Support or Pension Credit), so it is still worth claiming.

Sometimes, if you are paid Carer's Allowance, the person you care for may lose some of their benefit. If you are unsure, seek further advice.

To claim, call the Carer's Allowance Unit or the Benefits Enquiry Line (see chapter 6 for contact details) or claim online at www.direct.gov/carers.

CARER PREMIUM/ADDITION

The carer premium and addition are extra amounts used in the calculation of some means-tested benefits. The carer premium is used in Income Support, Jobseeker's Allowance, Housing Benefit and Council Tax Benefit and the carer addition is used in Pension Credit. The carer premium/addition is worth £27.15 per week (in the tax year 2007/8) and is included in your benefit calculations if you get Carer's Allowance or if you have 'underlying entitlement' to Carer's Allowance (see above).

PLANNING AHEAD

For every week Carer's Allowance is paid, you are credited with a National Insurance contribution. This helps to protect your entitlement to State Retirement Pension. If you are a carer but are not entitled to Carer's Allowance, you can claim Home Responsibilities Protection for every year you are a carer for at least 48 weeks. For more information about Home Responsibilities Protection contact the Pension Service (see chapter 6) or ask at your local Jobcentre Plus office.

LOOKING AFTER YOURSELF

'I couldn't do it by myself. I'd go bonkers. I'm lucky that my husband doesn't mind having Dad here so much. He takes him out sometimes just to give me a break.' (daughter)

When you are looking after someone else who is unwell or frail, it can be very easy to ignore your own needs. But if you do not maintain a life of your own, away from looking after your parent, you will probably become depressed and quite possibly ill. Wherever possible, try to share the load of caring with other family members and, if appropriate, friends of your parent. You may find it helpful to join a local carers' group for support, or, on the other hand, start a hobby or sport to take you away from your everyday worries.

Every day, make sure that you put aside some time for yourself – even if it is just to sit and have a cup of tea, read the paper, listen to some music or go for a walk. If your parent cannot be left alone, try to arrange for a friend, family member or sort out a rota for a variety of people to come round on a regular basis in order that you can get away from the house. Even if you are in your own home or that of your parent, you can become institutionalised if you fail to maintain some variety in your life. This is important for your parent as well as for you: they need you to maintain your morale and keep on top of things.

If your parent has had a Care Assessment and is deemed to need care, the local authority is obliged to arrange adequate help. Depending on your parent's financial position, this may need to be paid for but, even so, it is imperative that you have some time to yourself.

If you are at an early stage of caring for your parent, you should remember that it is not a passing phase but a commitment that may well become more demanding and last for a very long time. Although you may be managing with little outside help now, it is probable that the caring will become more challenging, both physically and emotionally. From the beginning you should:

- involve other family members so that the responsibility does not all rest with you. Even if they cannot offer help on a daily basis, they may be able to invite your parent for weekends or holidays or make a financial contribution to outside help.
- always try to accept help from friends or neighbours when they offer to lend a hand. If you get into the habit of saying that you are fine, they may think that you do not want their help and never make the offer again. Suggest ways in which they can help: take your parent for a walk, or sit and read to them, for example, so that you can get on with something else for a while.
- let people know that you value their support. Tell them how much your parent appreciates it when they pop in for a cup of tea or a chat.
- resist leading others to believe that it is no problem caring for your parent. Be honest about how much your life has changed as a result of having to take on the additional responsibility.

- make sure that you eat properly and regularly.
- take regular exercise and walk in the fresh air every day if at all possible.
- get enough sleep. If you have problems sleeping or if your parent needs help during the night, talk to your doctor about it. Arrange for help overnight if necessary, even if it is for just one or two nights a week.
- if your parent has problems standing up or walking around, make sure that you do not damage your back. Your GP should refer you to a community physiotherapist for advice. Also, a community occupational therapist should come to assess your parent's needs to see if there is any suitable equipment available to help them in the home (see 'Equipment for daily living', page 48).
- let your GP know if you start to feel depressed, anxious or worried about the future. These problems are easier to tackle at an early stage.

YOUR FINANCIAL SITUATION

If you have had to give up your job or reduce your working hours to look after your parent, you should be eligible for a Carer's Allowance (see page 29).

If you are living with your parent, check on your position and rights with regard to home and finances if your parent moves permanently into a care home or dies.

CONFLICTING DEMANDS

Try to pace yourself – you can only do so much. If you have a family of your own you may well feel torn between looking after them and looking after your parent as well as perhaps coping with the demands of a full-time job.

At times, caring can feel like a thankless task, especially if your parent seems to resent what you are trying to do for them and your partner and children resent the amount of time your parent demands.

You can only do your best, though, and there are limits to what one person can manage. It is to be hoped that your family will recognise this, be grateful for the efforts you make and offer help. If they do not, ask for it. You deserve their support and their praise.

RESPITE CARE

'I love Mum dearly, but we need to have some time to ourselves, and although it's a bit regimented, the home isn't bad.' (*daughter*)

'I need more help if my daughter goes away but get on well enough with the girls that come in to help.' (*father*)

If your parent needs a lot of looking after and you are the person doing most of the work, you can often carry on without realising how tired, worn-out and tense you become. It is important for you to have a break – whole days without having to worry about your parent. It can help you relax and recharge your batteries, and it will give you more patience as well as energy when you take up your caring duties again.

It is crucial for your own well-being that you have regular breaks, make time for your own needs and perhaps have a holiday with your own family or with another relative or friend. Respite care may also be needed in other situations. For example, you or one of your other family members might have to go into hospital.

FEELING GUILTY

Many people who care for a parent feel worried or guilty about taking a break; they fear that their parent will not be looked after properly or will feel unloved, even if the break is for a short period.

But you must remember that your parent will want you to have a life of your own as well as caring for them, and that if you carry on until you become ill or depressed you may become unable to look after them at all. Sometimes, when an older person becomes frail and unwell, they may also be awkward and say they do not want you to go away or have someone else in to help them and that they will manage on their own if necessary. When this happens, you need to remind yourself that they are not being reasonable, and that if they were fit and healthy they would recognise this.

If your parent has dementia (see pages 141–4), there is the added trauma for you to watch your parent become less and less the person they once were. It can be helpful to talk to professionals with knowledge about dementia or with other carers who are also looking after someone with a similar condition. The Alzheimer's Helpline can offer advice (see chapter 6 for details).

When you have decided that you need a break, if possible discuss the situation with your parent to see what sort of arrangement they would prefer. But do not be dissuaded from getting the respite.

CARE AT HOME

If your parent is feeling vulnerable and also if they have dementia, there are advantages in arranging for care at home. Older people usually find it reassuring to remain in familiar surroundings. On the other hand, unless your parent (or you as the carer) has had a Care Assessment and is deemed eligible for additional care, you might have to spend a lot of time and money to ensure that a suitable carer can come to stay.

In this situation, the easiest solution is probably to ask another family member or a close friend to stay. If that is not possible, there are a number of other options (see box). Note that full-time nursing care is usually very expensive and in any case may not be necessary.

Check your parent's household insurance to see that it includes cover for public liability in case anyone looking after your parent falls and hurts themselves. If you are paying someone directly, make sure that you have agreed in writing exactly what the fee is and what is to be provided for that fee. It is also important that the person is registered as self-employed so that you do not become liable for National Insurance payments as if you were their employer.

FINDING SOMEONE TO PROVIDE CARE AT HOME

Possibilities might include:

- personal recommendations – perhaps a fellow carer, the GP surgery or the local carers' support group may know of someone suitable
- home care agencies, which can find people to provide respite care. The local authority should have a list of registered local home care agencies
- a variety of help – if your parent does not need support 24 hours a day, a rota involving family, friends or neighbours, social services and voluntary agencies and even some private care might be the answer.

DETAILS FOR YOUR PARENT'S CARE

If you are going away, leave clear instructions for the individual or team who will be looking after your parent. These should include their daily routine, and exactly what help they may require and what medicines they should take. You should also leave the doctor's phone number and your own or that of someone else who can be contacted in case of emergency. Listing all this may take a while, but once it is done the instructions can be used on future occasions with just a check that your parent's medication or daily routine has not changed.

CARE IN A RESIDENTIAL HOME

Another option is short-term care provided by a residential care home, hospice or hospital. This is not always easy to arrange as it depends on a place being vacant at a specific time. However, some homes, hospices and hospitals put aside a number of places for short-term care, enabling carers to plan ahead.

Your parent's GP surgery should have some details of appropriate residential homes. If your parent has a Care Assessment and Care Plan, their care manager should be able to offer advice.

When arranging a short-term stay in a residential home, visit it beforehand and, if at all possible, take your parent with you. This way, both you and they can make sure that it is suitable. Away from city centres, many residential homes are set in fine gardens and could offer a good holiday to your parent at the same time as giving you a break.

PAYING FOR SHORT-TERM CARE

If your parent has had a Care Assessment, discuss the method of payment with their care manager. Broadly, if an older person has savings or a reasonable income, they will probably have to pay the full cost of short-term care. Homes providing nursing care are generally more expensive than homes providing residential care only. However, fees for either vary greatly so it is a good idea to approach several homes.

LOCAL AUTHORITY ARRANGEMENTS

If your parent has been assessed as needing and qualifying for short-term care, the local authority may provide it. However, if your parent can afford it, they will still need to contribute towards the cost.

The local authority can charge for short-term stays in care homes (of under eight weeks) in one of two ways. They can either assess the amount your parent should pay based on their income and capital, or they can charge what they think is a 'reasonable' amount, although this should take account of your parent's circumstances. If care is provided in a person's own home the local authority can ask your parent to pay 'a reasonable amount' towards the cost. Discuss with the Care Manager what contribution 'a reasonable amount' would be in your parent's case.

NHS ARRANGEMENTS

In some cases, the NHS may be able to provide short-term care, particularly if your parent is terminally ill. You should check with their GP. There is no charge for NHS services but benefits are sometimes affected by inpatient stays. Pages 180–5 of this book discuss going into hospital; also, your parent's local benefits agency or Citizens Advice Bureau will have information about this. ■

2

CHOOSING WHERE YOUR PARENTS WILL LIVE

CHOOSING WHERE YOUR PARENTS WILL LIVE

'When we do need help, we would prefer to move into sheltered accommodation rather than put strain on family relationships.' (*mother*)

'After 60 years of marriage, I think it's inhumane to expect my 81-year-old father to live alone.' (*daughter*)

'We would not voluntarily leave our home even if our health deteriorated. We chose our house because it is easy to manage and we are close to the city centre and shops, all accessible by bus.' (*father*)

In recent generations, families have dispersed as children have grown up and moved away from the parental home. Whereas, 50 years ago, adult children often lived within easy reach of their elderly parents, today they are as likely to live at the other end of the country or abroad as to live in their home town. In many countries it is assumed that an ageing parent will move in with one of their children and perhaps, as in parts of southern Europe, subsequently spend lengthy periods at the homes of other children. However, in the UK this is not the case. Not only do most adult children expect their parents to live independently for as long as possible, but most of those parents expect and hope that they will do so.

Sooner or later, though, a parent will need more help. Perhaps also, and often as a result of widowhood, he or she will be facing desperate loneliness. Somehow, after a lifetime of living with family, children and a spouse, we expect our oldest generation to learn to live alone – and so do they.

WEIGHING UP THE OPTIONS

Whether your parent is planning to stay at home, move into a care home or sheltered accommodation, or move in with you or another member of the family, learning more about what is available will allow them to make an informed decision about the sort of housing best suited to their needs.

Many people want to carry on living in their own home. But staying put does not mean that things have to stay the same. Encourage your parent to think about whether their house still meets their needs, or whether there are any changes that will make life easier. Issues to consider include security and safety, repairs and improvements, support in the home and help with money.

SECURITY AND SAFETY

A key part of being happy in your own home is to be free of worries about security and safety. If your parent is concerned about home security contact their local police station and ask for a visit from the crime prevention officer, who can advise on making the home more secure.

The crime prevention officer can also tell your parent if there is a Neighbourhood Watch scheme in the area. Some Neighbourhood Watch schemes have regular meetings, which may offer an opportunity for your parent to get out and get to know their neighbours better.

Through the Help the Aged HandyVan service, older people who meet the Charity's financial criteria can have home safety and security devices fitted free of charge (see chapter 6 for contact details).

Being able to summon help in an emergency is also important. If you worry about your parent having an accident or falling ill while alone at home, you might want to think about arranging for them to have a community alarm.

A community alarm allows vulnerable people to call for help even if they cannot get to a phone; a 24-hour response centre is contacted by pressing a button on a pendant or wristband that your parent could wear all the time. Staff at the centre will then call out the best person to help – you perhaps, or a neighbour, relative or friend or, if necessary, the emergency services.

Many local authorities run their own community alarm schemes; contact the housing department of your parent's local council for information. Help the Aged runs its own 24-hour immediate telephone response service (like a community alarm scheme) called SeniorLink (or CareLine in Northern Ireland). You can buy or rent a SeniorLink unit, or Help the Aged may be able to supply your parent with one if your parent is on a low income. For more information, contact SeniorLink (see chapter 6).

REPAIRS, IMPROVEMENTS AND ADAPTATIONS

Your parent's home may need some repairs to make it safer or more comfortable. If they own their home and have savings, this will probably be their own responsibility. It is essential to find a reliable firm to carry out the work. Get your parent to make a detailed list of what they think is needed and discuss it with them. If you think they have overlooked something, remember that it is your parent who will continue to live in the house, not you. Nevertheless, gently remind them of anything that seems to you to need attention. When they are ready to get quotes for the work, encourage them to get at least three written quotations from different companies.

If possible, approach builders who have done work for someone your family knows and trusts, and who belong to a respected trade organisation such as the Federation of Master Builders. If you do not know the business, check the address of the building firm and ask them to show you some recent customer references. Finally, make sure that all the details of the work to be done, the timings and the costs are agreed in writing. Do not let your parent be pressured into having building work done by doorstep traders.

The Office of Fair Trading produces a booklet, *Home Improvements*, which gives useful guidance on planning and managing work. See chapter 6 for the address.

ADVICE FOR TENANTS

If your parent is a housing association or private tenant, the landlord is usually responsible for carrying out necessary repairs. If you are concerned that repairs are not being made, ask your parent to check their rent book or tenancy agreement to see whether this is the case. If the landlord is not responsible, then your parent can apply for a council grant (see below).

If your parent is a council tenant, many repairs will be the council's responsibility. They should then contact the housing department of the local council (or the local housing executive in Northern Ireland) to find out how to get repairs done.

If your parent's landlord is unwilling to make repairs they are responsible for, seek advice from the local Citizens Advice Bureau or the council's housing advice centre.

GRANTS FROM THE COUNCIL

Your parent may be able to get a grant or loan from the local council to help with the costs of small repairs to their home and major renovation work: for example, replacing a rotten window or installing a bathroom if they do not have one. If your parent is disabled they can also apply for a grant to adapt their home to make it easier to live in: this could include having ramps and grab rails fitted, and devices to make it easier to use the bathroom.

The help available will depend on finances, where your parent lives, and whether they are a home owner or a tenant. Your parent's local Citizens Advice Bureau or home improvement agency should be able to give you advice on the grants available in the area.

Bear in mind that even if your parent is eligible for a grant, it can be quite difficult to arrange, depending on the financial situation and policies of the local council. But it is always worth trying. Also, ensure that work is not started until the grant has been approved, otherwise the council can refuse to pay any grant at all.

INSULATION AND DRAUGHT-PROOFING

Good insulation and draught-proofing can make a big difference both to comfort and to fuel bills. Although there are often waiting lists, grants are available throughout the UK to help pay for this. Depending on where your parent lives, telephone one of the numbers listed under 'Insulation and draught-proofing' in chapter 6 for further information about what is available and how long they may have to wait.

OTHER SOURCES OF FUNDING

If your parent cannot get a grant, or if they are given one that covers only part of the cost, they may want to look at other ways of raising money.

They could consider borrowing money against their home through an ordinary loan, or an interest-only loan. With an interest-only loan they would only pay back interest each month: the sum they borrow does not have to be repaid until the house is sold. Before considering any sort of loan, they should think carefully about whether they can afford the repayments. With an ordinary loan, they should remember that monthly repayments will probably be high as it will be repaid over a relatively short period. They may be able to claim for some repairs on their house insurance. Day-to-day repair work is not usually covered, but things like storm damage to roofs or subsidence might be.

If your parent owns their own home they may want to consider an equity release scheme, which involves mortgaging or selling part of their home in return for a cash lump sum or a regular monthly income.

It is important to get professional advice if your parent is seriously thinking about taking out an equity release scheme or loan. Help the Aged has a free information sheet on its website about equity release, and also runs a dedicated advice service (see chapter 6) for those who wish to explore the possibilities.

SOCIAL FUND PAYMENTS

If your parent needs a small amount of work done and is receiving Pension Credit, they could apply for a Social Fund Community Care Grant. These can be given towards the cost of minor essential repairs and improvements, furniture and equipment. Payments are discretionary, which means that there is no legal right to a grant.

If your parent has been getting Pension Credit for at least six months they may be able to get a Social Fund Budgeting Loan. These are paid out of their weekly Pension Credit. But bear in mind that Budgeting Loans can result in more debt and difficulty. It is always better to try to get a grant.

Contact your parent's local social security office for more information on applying for a Social Fund grant or loan.

GIFTED HOUSING (HELP THE AGED)

If your parent owns their home and is thinking about leaving their estate, or part of it, to a charity, they could consider the Help the Aged Gifted Housing service. In return for donating their property to Help the Aged, the Charity takes responsibility for repairs and maintenance, property insurance, Council Tax and water rates; provides a community alarm; and helps with gardening costs. Your parent would just pay the fuel and telephone bills and contents insurance. The Gifted Housing team can also help with arranging and paying for care. Contact details are in chapter 6.

MOVING TO A NEW HOME

If your parent is considering moving house, encourage them to think carefully about their reasons before committing. Perhaps their home is now too big, or is expensive to run. Maybe they want to be closer to family, or want a home that is all on one level.

But will a new home meet all their expectations? For example, if they want to move to the seaside town where they spend their holidays, will things seem quite so positive in the middle of winter when

POINTS TO CONSIDER BEFORE MOVING HOUSE

- **Layout and size** Is the arrangement and size of the rooms convenient? Is there a downstairs toilet? Is there a spare room for visitors and enough storage space?
- **Upkeep and maintenance** Will the house be easy to look after? Does it need any major repairs? Is it well insulated? Does it have effective heating?
- **Location** Is the property close to the shops, post office, library and other facilities your parent uses regularly? Are there good public transport links? Is the area noisy? Has your parent visited the area at night to get an idea of how safe it seems?
- **Cost** Will the move make your parents better or worse off? As well as the rent or mortgage (if required), other things to consider include Council Tax, maintenance costs and service charges.

Northern Ireland has a rates system, whereby every property is valued individually, instead of Council Tax. If your parent lives in Northern Ireland or wants to live there, they should contact the rebate section of the rate collection agency in the local area for details.

they are a long way from friends (and possibly family) and the shops and facilities they have known for a long while?

Many options are available if your parent does decide to move: a different house; sheltered accommodation; moving into a care home; living with family. Other possibilities include everything from moving to a caravan or 'park home', to emigrating to a country with a warmer climate.

Whatever your parent wants to do, they should seek advice before making a decision. Elderly Accommodation Counsel offers a comprehensive advice service covering all types of housing for older people.

MOVING HOUSE

If your parent is thinking about moving house, it is important to look to the future. Will their new home be suitable in the longer term? It may be useful for your parent to consider some of the points listed in the box (previous page), and whether they want to buy or rent.

There are of course many other questions that your parent will want to ask. They may find it useful to talk to prospective neighbours to get their impression of the area.

If your parent is a council tenant and wants to move within the same area, they should contact the local housing department (or housing executive in Northern Ireland) and ask for a transfer. Although there are often long waiting lists, they may have more chance if they want to move out of a larger 'family' home into a smaller one.

If your parent wants to move to a different area, an organisation called Move UK might be able to help. Move UK can help council tenants through its Mobility Scheme or the Homeswap exchange scheme. Your parent should ask their housing department for details or contact Move UK directly.

If your parent is a housing association tenant, ask the association whether it has any suitable accommodation in the area they want to move to. It is possible that the housing association is involved with one of the Move UK schemes.

Difficulties can arise if your parents own their home but want to move into council or housing association rented accommodation. Councils and housing associations have long waiting lists, and councils in particular may not consider home owners for rehousing. However, if there are strong reasons why you feel such a move is necessary for your parent's well-being, talk to the local council to see if it can help. It might be easier if your parent wants to move specifically into sheltered housing.

MOVING IN WITH FAMILY

Your parent may be considering moving into your home or with another member of your family (or perhaps have family members come to live in their home). If so, everyone needs to think carefully about their expectations and how things would work.

One major consideration, which is sometimes forgotten, is whether your parent actually gets on with the people they intend to live with. If they do not all get on well at the moment, while living apart, it is unlikely things will get much better when they are always in each other's company.

It is particularly important to get legal advice if your parent is selling his current home and/or putting money towards buying a house with another member of the family. Although it might seem awkward or untrusting to seek independent advice, it is better for everyone in the long term that everyone is sure of their position before committing themselves.

The implications of having your parent live with you are discussed in further detail in the section 'Living with you', pages 92–6.

EQUIPMENT FOR THE HOME

'I was imprisoned in the house until I decided to buy a scooter so that I could get out short distances, which I love.' (*mother*)

'After I broke my arm, the OT [occupational therapist] came and assessed what I could do and what I needed.' (*mother*)

Many different aids and adaptations are available to help older people continue living in their own home. For example, if they find it difficult to get in and out of the bath, a grab rail or a special bath seat might help.

Adaptations to doorways in their house can enable them to use a wheelchair more easily. There are also hundreds of simple gadgets which can help with daily tasks like cooking, washing, dressing, using the toilet and bathing: equipment for daily living.

EQUIPMENT FOR DAILY LIVING

This is the general name for all the aids and adaptations that can help older people to continue living in their own homes. There are also hundreds of simple gadgets that can help them perform everyday tasks easily and safely. As they are not usually found in high street shops, neither you nor your parent may realise just what is available. Some examples of the gadgets and equipment your parent might find useful are given below.

In the bathroom:
- grab rails and bath seats to help people climb in and out of the bath;
- special seats that fix to the wall so people can have showers sitting down;
- raised toilet seats that make getting on to and off the toilet a lot easier;
- long-handled sponges, hairbrushes and make-up sponges to make daily hygiene and beauty routines easier to manage.

In the kitchen:
- 'spike boards' to hold vegetables for chopping;
- non-slip mats to keep a plate still when cutting up food;
- kettle and teapot 'tippers' that make it easy to pour safely;
- sliding shelves to make it easier to help reach the back of cupboards;
- jar openers to take the strain out of opening stiff jar tops;
- electric can openers that make opening cans easier;
- plastic tap turners to help turn stiff taps on and off.

In the bedroom:
- 'bed raisers' that fit on to the feet of a bed, giving it extra height;
- simple aids to help people pull themselves into a sitting position in bed;
- button-fasteners and zip-pullers to make getting dressed easier;

- dressing sticks for putting on and taking off stockings, tights, trousers, shirts and socks without having to bend.

In the living room:

- manually and electrically operated reclining chairs to help people sit upright or lie back, and also to push them forward and support them while they stand up;
- 'chair raisers' that fit on to the legs of chairs, giving them added height;
- long-handled window openers to help people reach high window catches;
- large-print books, for people with poor sight; books, newspapers and magazines are also available on audiotape from libraries and specialist organisations such as the RNIB (Royal National Institute for the Blind) Talking Book Service, Calibre Audio Library and the Talking Newspaper Association (see chapter 6 for contact details). Audio (or 'talking') books are also available to buy.

Around the house:

- special handles to fit on to plugs to take the strain out of pulling them out of sockets;
- long-handled 'grabbers' to help pick things up from the floor or take them from high shelves;
- telephones with large buttons for people with poor sight;
- telephones that have a flashing light instead of a ringing tone for people with poor hearing.

FINDING OUT ABOUT EQUIPMENT FOR DAILY LIVING

If you would like more information and advice on the different types of gadgets available, a number of organisations can help. You can find contact details for all the organisations mentioned in this section in chapter 6.

The Disabled Living Foundation (see chapter 6) operates a telephone and letter advice service on all types of disability equipment, clothing and footwear. It can suggest what equipment might best suit your parent's needs, and give details of local suppliers. It also runs an online service for older and disabled people called 'bathing made easy'.

The national research charity Ricability (the Research Institute for Consumer Affairs) produces a range of independent consumer reports that offer practical information and advice for older and disabled people on choosing products and services. Topics covered by the guides include telephones, easier living in the home, buying or upgrading central heating controls, community alarms, driving and car adaptations. Contact Ricability for a publications list or visit its website to download the reports.

If you think it would be a good idea for your parent to try out different types of equipment, you can arrange for them to visit a local Disabled Living Centre. There are many Disabled Living Centres around the UK where all sorts of equipment from simple gadgets to larger items of equipment such as wheelchairs can be tried.

You can find your parent's nearest Disabled Living Centre by contacting Assist UK, Disability Wales or Disability Action in Northern Ireland. There may also be a demonstration centre for disability equipment run by your parent's local council or hospital occupational therapy department.

For advice on the special equipment available for people with sight problems, contact the Royal National Institute for the Blind (RNIB) and the Partially Sighted Society (see chapter 6).

RNID and Hearing Concern can both give information on equipment for people who are hard of hearing.

If there is nothing at all available for your parent's particular difficulty, two organisations that may be able to help are Remap and DEMAND (see chapter 6) – charities that design and build special equipment to meet one-off needs. The equipment they make is given to the disabled person free of charge.

LOCAL AUTHORITY AND NHS EQUIPMENT

Your parent's local authority or the NHS may provide some equipment and adaptations. A local authority can provide things like: grab rails, stair lifts, 'raisers' to make chairs and beds higher, raised toilet seats and bath seats.

Your parent will need to have a needs assessment (see 'Care assessment', page 18). An occupational therapist may visit to give expert advice on what equipment will be suitable. However, the local authority will have set rules about who qualifies for the equipment available. If your parent would be at risk if they do not have the equipment provided they will have a greater chance of qualifying for help.

Some equipment, such as continence equipment and commodes, can be provided through the NHS. You should contact your parent's GP surgery to find out how they can help. If your parent has had an assessment from the local authority they should be able to get help to get the necessary health equipment.

The local British Red Cross may loan out disability equipment such as wheelchairs and commodes. But you will probably find that they need your parent to be referred to them by a social worker or a health professional.

GETTING HELP FROM THE LOCAL COUNCIL AND THE NHS

The occupational therapist will help your parent find a solution by looking at different ways in which they can perform difficult tasks, and by suggesting the most suitable equipment. The occupational therapist will then usually arrange for the equipment your parent needs to be provided, but it may not be free.

MOBILITY AIDS

If your parent needs a walking stick or a walking frame, they should talk to their doctor, who will probably refer them to the physiotherapy or occupational therapy department of their local hospital.

If your parent needs a wheelchair, their doctor, physiotherapist or occupational therapist will refer them to the local NHS Wheelchair Service centre. The wheelchair will be free and fully maintained, although there may be no choice as to which wheelchair is provided. If your parent would prefer to get the wheelchair of their choice, they may be offered an NHS voucher which can be used to pay for it. If the voucher is not enough to cover the cost, your parent will have to make up the difference. If you are interested in buying a powered wheelchair for your parent, always check that the voucher will be valid.

To facilitate mobility away from the house, your parent may choose to purchase a scooter. Some mobility scooters need to be registered with the Driver and Vehicle Licensing Agency (DVLA). If your parent requires a class 3 scooter which is capable of exceeding speeds of 4mph but not more than 8mph, it will need to be registered with the DVLA. It will be licensed in the 'disabled' taxation class and display a nil-duty tax disc. It will not need evidence of Vehicle Excise Duty (VED) exemption or payment of the first registration fee. It will not need to display registration plates either. Class 2 scooters, which cannot exceed 4mph and are intended for use only on pathways, do not have to be registered.

It may be worth considering insurance for such a mobility aid. It is not a legal requirement to have insurance for powered wheelchairs, scooters or buggies. But it could be a good idea to have at least public liability insurance, which covers accidental damage to property and other people. Your parent might also consider insurance that covers the equipment in the event of theft, fire or other damage. It might be possible to add the mobility aid to a home contents policy. Alternatively, Motability – a car scheme for disabled people – has an insurance plan for disabled people called the Motability Wheelchair Insurance Plan (see contact details in chapter 6).

Your parent may only need a wheelchair or other mobility aid for a short period of time. If this is the case, the British Red Cross may be able to help. It operates a medical loan service that can supply wheelchairs and other mobility aids on a temporary basis.

HOME NURSING EQUIPMENT
This is a general term covering items which are needed to help with certain medical conditions, such as continence pads, commodes and plastic sheets. Your parent's district nurse will usually arrange the sup-

ply of this equipment. The equipment available on the NHS varies from one district to another and, depending on where your parent lives, they may have to pay for certain items, such as continence pads. To find out whether your parent will be charged for continence pads speak to the local NHS specialist continence service. Call the Continence Foundation (see chapter 6) to find out how to contact your parent's local service.

If your parent needs equipment such as a commode or bedpan only for a short period of time, it might be worth contacting the British Red Cross, which may be able to supply you with the equipment you need through its medical loan service.

BUYING EQUIPMENT FROM PRIVATE COMPANIES

If your parent's local social services department (social work department in Scotland; health and social services trust in Northern Ireland) cannot supply the equipment required or your parent is not eligible to get equipment from their local authority or the NHS, they might want to consider buying their own. The Disabled Living Foundation, a charity, can give impartial advice and information on different aids and equipment. It can also provide lists of suppliers. See chapter 6 for the helpline number.

Some companies will sell disability equipment to people in their own home. This can be very convenient, as you can see how the equipment will work *in situ*. However, there have been reports of people receiving an unsatisfactory service and it may be a good idea to be with your parents if a sales representative is calling. Be aware that some companies sell over-priced equipment to older people which they do not really need. Some doorstep sellers put people under a lot of pressure to buy their products without giving them a chance to try them out. For example, people have been sold electric scooters that will not fit through their front door.

Not only is disability equipment vital for your parent's independence, it can also be expensive, so make sure that your parent thinks very carefully before signing a contract. If your parent signs a contract with a salesperson whom they have invited into their home, but then changes their mind or finds out that the equipment does not suit them, they may not be able to cancel the contract without losing money. So they need to be certain about what they need before making a commitment.

SECOND-HAND EQUIPMENT

If your parent is buying second-hand equipment it is essential to check that it is in good working order and that it will suit their needs. The seller must give an accurate description of the equipment, including any faults, before your parent buys. It is best to get this in writing: this will make it easier for your parent to get their money back if they find any faults that they were not told about. It is also important to get hold of the equipment's user manual and safety instructions.

If your parent is interested in buying or selling second-hand equipment contact the Disability Equipment Register. Your parent's local Disabled Living Centre may also know of second-hand equipment for sale in the area. Some companies buy and sell second-hand equipment, which may come with a limited guarantee.

FINANCIAL HELP

Many gadgets and aids, because of their simplicity, are relatively cheap to buy. However, some disability equipment can be expensive. If your parent cannot afford to buy what they need, they may be able to get financial help.

The Government is keen for older people to stay living in their own homes rather than move into a care home or a hospital. Community Care Grants are available for people who want to stay living independently in the community. To apply, your parent must be receiving Pension Credit and have less than £1,000 savings. They will be expected to use any savings over £1,000 to pay for whatever equipment they need. Application forms for the grants are available from the local benefits office. These are discretionary grants, so your parent cannot be certain of getting one, but it is worth applying.

If your parent needs help making the application and you are unable to assist them, the local Citizens Advice Bureau might be able to help.

ADAPTING YOUR PARENT'S HOME

Some people find that, even with equipment and aids, they still have difficulties living in their home. If your parent is in this situation they may need to think about making some adaptations. Adaptations range from installing a stair lift or grab rails to making a home suitable for someone who uses a wheelchair. The Disabled Living Foundation and the Centre for Accessible Environments can give advice on what adaptations might be possible. Your parent might be able to get a grant from the local council to help with the costs. To find out, contact their local Home Improvement Agency.

HELP AND ADVICE ON REPAIRS AND IMPROVEMENTS

Home improvement agencies (HIAs) provide older home owners and private tenants with help and advice on repairs, improvements and adaptations. Often called Care and Repair or Staying Put agencies, they are non-profit-making and usually run by local authorities and housing associations. There is an HIA in most areas.

If there is an agency in your parent's area that can help, someone will visit to discuss their housing problems and will then help to organise whatever work is needed. They will also help to sort out the financial side. Home improvement agencies have different names in different areas: see under 'H' in chapter 6 for contact details relevant to your parent's area:

CARE IN YOUR PARENT'S HOME

'I have a wonderful helper who cleans the house twice a week, rings me each morning to wake me up, makes my high tea and makes my bed. I love my children but I don't want to live with any, as much for their sake as mine.' (*mother*)

'I would dread having to enter sheltered housing or a care home, but would consider pooling abilities and finances with a friend. I would not want to live with a child or other relative.' (*mother*)

'It's a shame that the carers who go into Mum change a lot. She sometimes gets confused as to who's been there.' (*daughter*)

'My mother insists on her independence and is often very rude to the carers.' (*son*)

'I take every opportunity of help from Age Concern. They organise outings and deliver daily meals.' (*mother*)

Many older people prefer to stay independent in their own homes for as long as possible even if they need some help to do so, whether for domestic tasks or personal care. Current government policy positively encourages this but it is not always easy to see what support is available for older people or their carers.

The following is a guide to help you find out what help may be appropriate and how to go about getting it. But you should also consider whether loneliness will become an issue if your parent lives alone in their own home. Even with adequate care, if your parent lives far from friends and family and is no longer mobile, isolation may become a big problem that can lead to depression. Find out from the local council about any appropriate social activities that may be available locally, such as lunch clubs, book clubs, bingo or faith groups.

LOCAL AUTHORITY AND NHS SERVICES

Local authority social services departments are responsible for arranging services which help older and disabled people stay in their own homes, while the NHS focuses on health issues and therapy.

If your parent needs help from the local social services depart-

LOCAL AUTHORITY SERVICES

The local authority can provide help with activities such as:

- getting in and out of bed
- bathing and washing
- preparing meals
- shopping
- cleaning
- equipment and adaptations to the home, such as grab rails and bath seats.

NHS SERVICES

The NHS can provide help with:

- continence advice and equipment
- chiropody/podiatry (but note that service provision in many areas is extremely poor)
- occupational therapy
- physiotherapy
- medical equipment, such as wheelchairs and special beds.

ment or NHS they will be required to have an assessment of their needs (see 'Care assessment', page 18).

WHAT HELP WILL MY PARENT GET?

Once your parent's needs have been assessed they should be given a care plan, explaining what services can be provided for them and how they will be provided. If the local authority assesses your parent as needing services, there are several ways in which it can meet this need. It can:

- directly provide its own services;
- arrange for services to be provided by voluntary organisations and private agencies;
- give your parent cash to arrange and manage their own

care: this is known as Direct Payments (see below for more information).

The 'care package' could include services from a number of organisations. For example:

- social services may provide grab rails for the bathroom;
- the WRVS might provide meals on wheels;
- a private agency might come in and help your parent to get up in the mornings; and
- your parent could have a place in a day centre run by a local voluntary group such as Age Concern.

But whoever provides the services, social services is still responsible for ensuring that they are right for your parent and that their needs are being met.

If you become aware of any problems with the services you should contact your parent's care manager.

If your parent needs help outside office hours, you can telephone the main social services number and a message will give the number of a duty social worker. If urgent help is required or your parent has a crisis, you can always contact someone at social services.

WILL MY PARENT GET ALL THE HELP THEY NEED?

Unfortunately, because social services and the NHS have a limited amount of money to spend on services, they often ration the amount of help they give. This could mean that your parent might not be offered all the services you think they need. When it decides what services it will provide, the local authority is allowed to set its own rules ('eligibility criteria') about whom it will help. These eligibility criteria should be available to you on request.

The local authority can also limit the amount of help it will give anyone at home to no more than it would cost to pay for a place in a care home. However, if there are special reasons why you think your parent should stay at home the local authority should take these into account.

If you feel that your parent has not been offered enough

services to meet their needs you can make a complaint.

DIRECT PAYMENTS

Your parent might have the option to arrange their own care with cash provided by the local authority, instead of receiving services. You may choose to become involved with this decision. This system is called Direct Payments. Direct Payments allow your parent to decide who cares for them and how the money is spent.

The rules about who can get Direct Payments are different in each country. But all local authorities now have a duty to offer the option of Direct Payments to:

- disabled people; and
- anyone aged 65 or over who has been assessed as needing community care services.

They also have to offer Direct Payments to carers (except in Scotland, where this duty extends only to carers of disabled children).

Your parent's local authority will have to be satisfied that you and your parent are capable of handling Direct Payments alone or with assistance. They will expect detailed accounts of how the money is spent.

Remember, just because a Direct Payment arrangement is offered does not mean that you or your parent has to accept it. If your parent prefers, they can have their care arranged by the local authority.

What can Direct Payments be used for?

Direct Payments can be used to buy any services that will meet your parent's 'assessed needs', as detailed on the Care Assessment. This includes help with personal care and daily tasks: for example, bathing and going to the toilet, respite care, and equipment (such as grab rails). The local council will need to be satisfied that what your parent is spending their Direct Payments on meets their 'assessed needs'.

Your parent can use their Direct Payments to employ their own staff to carry out the services they require, or they can choose to buy services from voluntary or private agencies.

Employing staff

You parent can use Direct Payments to employ their own care workers, also known as 'personal assistants' (someone who helps with everyday tasks such as getting dressed, cooking, getting around and reminding your parent to take their medicines). Employing their own staff may offer your parent greater flexibility about the precise kind of help they want and when they want it. It can also mean that there will be more continuity in care, because the same people will be supporting your parent all the time.

Your parent would not usually be able to use Direct Payments to pay a spouse or close relative who lives with them, although exceptions can be made to this rule if it is considered necessary to meet the older person's needs. If your parent lives in Scotland they can only use Direct Payments to pay for services from a spouse, partner or close relative if that person does not live at the same address.

If your parent decides to employ their own staff they will need to deal with issues such as recruitment, tax and National Insurance. You may wish to help them and will need to make sure that they have third-party liability insurance, in case the carer or personal assistant has an accident while working. You will also have to manage issues such as wages and holidays for the staff. Various organisations can offer help with this aspect of Direct Payments (see chapter 6).

Your parent should also be able to get support from the local council if they want to employ their own personal assistants or care workers. For example, social services may be able to explain how to keep records or direct them to a payroll service.

There may also be a local Direct Payments support service, which can help you and your parent through all the stages of getting and looking after Direct Payments. These support services are user-led and usually run by voluntary organisations, such as a local disability organisation or Age Concern. They can:

- give information and advice on how the scheme works;
- help your parent to decide whether it is suitable for their needs;

- help your parent complete the application forms and other paperwork;
- help your parent to find someone to work for them or to choose an agency.

Direct Payments support services often hold regular user meetings where your parent can meet other users and discuss any matters that concern them. Following the Care Assessment, your parent will be designated a care manager who should be able to give details of the local Direct Payments support service if they decide this is what they want.

If your parent does decide to employ staff, they will also need to think about getting cover for holidays and emergencies. For example, if they employ a personal assistant who helps them to get up in the morning, what will happen if that person is taken ill? It is worth discussing this with your parent's care manager and finding out what arrangements can be made for emergency cover.

Your parent should always be able to contact social services in an emergency. If something unexpected happens and they have no cover, they or you should contact the local council. It should step in to make sure your parent has the services required. If your parent needs help outside office hours, they should telephone the main social services number and a message will give the number of a duty social worker.

BUYING CARE SERVICES FROM A VOLUNTARY OR PRIVATE AGENCY

If your parent prefers, they can make a contract with a voluntary or private agency, using the Direct Payments to buy care and support services from them.

This means that they will not have the same responsibilities that they would have if they were directly employing someone. For example, they will not have to worry about National Insurance, holiday pay and so on.

See box overleaf for how to find an agency.

FINDING A CARE AGENCY

There are a various ways in which you can find a local care agency for your parent:

■ The UK Home Care Association can give details of home care providers who follow its code of practice. It also produces a useful leaflet, *Choosing Care in Your Home*. See chapter 6 for contact details.

■ You may be able to get details of approved private agencies from your local social services department. Ask for the company registration department.

■ You may be able to get a recommendation from a friend or relative; or check your phonebook for local agencies.

The charity Counsel and Care (see chapter 6) produces a factsheet called *What to Look For in a Home Care Agency*.

CARE STANDARDS

All agencies that provide care at home should be registered with a care standards authority. This means that they have to abide by national minimum care standards. Care standards cover a range of issues from legal rights to a written care plan and contract, to a person's rights to privacy and dignity.

VOLUNTARY HELP

Many voluntary organisations provide services such as visiting, meals on wheels, shopping, gardening and transport schemes.

To get help from voluntary organisations, contact them directly. However, some services will want your parent to be referred by social services.

Some of the voluntary organisations that provide help at home are listed below (see chapter 6 for contact details). Your parent's local library and telephone directory will also list voluntary groups in the locality.

- WRVS offers a choice of services including visiting schemes, shopping services, home-delivered meals, volunteer drivers and escort schemes in England, Scotland and Wales.
- Local Age Concerns offer a range of services provided by volunteers such as visiting, shopping and gardening.
- Crossroads schemes help carers by providing respite care attendants while they have a break. They may make a small charge for this service.

BUYING CARE SERVICES FROM YOUR LOCAL COUNCIL

If your parent lives in England, Wales or Northern Ireland, they cannot use Direct Payments to buy services from the local council. They will have to buy services from a voluntary or private agency. The Government is thinking about changing this rule in future. However, it is possible to have a combination of some services provided directly by social services and others arranged independently with Direct Payments. For example, your parent's local authority may provide grab rails for the bathroom; but your parent may choose to use Direct Payments to employ a carer to help them get up in the mornings.

If you think this would suit your parent best, ask social services if it will agree to do this.

Older people living in Scotland can use Direct Payments to buy services from their local council, or from another local council.

CARE HOMES AND DIRECT PAYMENTS

Direct Payments can only be used to pay for short, temporary stays in a care home; they cannot be used to pay for longer or permanent stays.

Your parent is allowed to use Direct Payments to stay in a care home for periods of up to four weeks at a time. If they are at home for 28 days or less between stays in a care home, the separate stays will be added together. In total, Direct Payments are not allowed to be used for stays in a care home for more than 120 days in a year.

HOW MUCH WILL MY PARENT GET TO PAY FOR CARE SERVICES?

Your parent's local council should always provide enough money to enable them to buy services that meet their basic 'assessed needs'. If you decide that you would like a more expensive service or extra help for your parent, there is nothing to stop you from 'topping up' your parent's Direct Payments with your own money or theirs, or, for example, money from a friend or a charity. But this should be a matter of choice: you should not be forced into doing this because the local council does not provide enough money.

If your parent chooses to employ their own care workers, they should receive enough to be able to fulfil their legal obligations as an employer. For example, the Direct Payment might include an amount to cover employer liability insurance, the personal assistant's National Insurance payments and statutory holiday and sick pay.

If you do not think that your parent has been offered enough money, you can help them make a complaint. While the complaint is being dealt with your parent can, for the time being, choose to:

- accept the Direct Payments that were offered; or
- receive services from the local council instead.

HOW MUCH WILL MY PARENT HAVE TO PAY FOR CARE SERVICES?

If your parent receives care services directly from the local council, they will work out how much needs to be contributed towards the cost. If your parent is getting Direct Payments instead of services, the contribution should be calculated in exactly the same way (see 'Paying for home care services', below).

Once the local council has worked out how much your parent should pay it will either:

- take this amount away from the Direct Payments before they are paid, with your parent's agreement; or
- pay your parent the whole amount: your parent will then have to pay their contribution to the local council.

WILL DIRECT PAYMENTS AFFECT MY PARENT'S BENEFITS?

Direct Payments are tax-free and will not affect benefits. However, benefits may be taken into account when your parent's local council is working out how much it can afford to pay towards the cost of the care (see below for more information).

PAYING FOR HOME CARE SERVICES

Once the local council has made the care assessment and decided what services are required, it will work out how much your parent should contribute towards the cost.

The rules on charging vary depending on which area of the UK your parent lives in.

The assessment of how much your parent should contribute should always come after their needs have been assessed. In other words, the services being offered should never be affected by how much your parent can afford to pay towards them.

The rules on funding are not always clear and can be complicated. If you would like advice on your parent's personal situation call the Help the Aged service SeniorLine (see chapter 6).

DISABILITY BENEFITS AND CARE SERVICES

Local councils can, if they want, treat most disability benefits as income. This includes Attendance Allowance (AA), the care component of Disability Living Allowance (DLA), and any extra Pension Credit your parent gets because of severe disability. But they should ignore the mobility component of Disability Living Allowance. Also, if your parent is only receiving daytime services, the council should not count any part of the AA or DLA that is paid for night care. (See 'Disability benefits', page 113.)

If your parent's disability benefits are counted as income, the local council should assess his or her 'disability-related expenditure'. This is the extra money they need to spend in order to live independently. Your parent's local council should take this expenditure into account when it is working out how much it should charge.

For example, your parent's disability could mean they need to pay for:

- privately arranged care services;
- special clothing or footwear;
- additional laundry costs;
- additional heating costs; or
- special dietary needs.

The local council should make sure that your parent is left with enough money to pay for this care and support.

The local council may decide to take into account any capital and savings your parent has. However, the value of your parent's home should not be counted as capital for non-residential care services.

What if your parent refuses to pay for services?

A local council should not withdraw a service because someone refuses to pay a charge. But it can pursue the debt through the civil courts.

If you or your parent do not agree with the amount charged, you can ask the decision to be reviewed or make a formal complaint. (See 'Local authority complaints', page 22.)

Intermediate care

Your parent should not be charged for any 'intermediate care' they receive. Intermediate care is a type of short-term rehabilitation and recovery service, intended to help the older person:

- recover their independence and get back to living at home if they have been in hospital; or
- maintain their independence by providing short-term intensive support so that they can avoid going into hospital.

Intermediate care is often only for one or two weeks and is normally limited to six weeks in total. It can be provided in a hospital or care home, or at your parent's own home. If the NHS provides intermediate care, it will be paid for by the NHS.

CARE SERVICES IN SCOTLAND

If your parent lives in Scotland and is aged 65 or over, they will not have to pay for any personal care services they are assessed as needing. However, they may have to pay towards other services, such as cleaning and shopping. This will depend on the charging policy of the local council. If they are under 65, the local council will work out how much they should contribute towards all of the care services.

Your parent's local council should be able to supply information on what services 'personal care' includes, and on the local eligibility criteria for these services.

However, in general, personal care covers:

- help with washing, bathing and trimming nails;
- help with going to the toilet or using a bedpan;
- help with the use of continence equipment, such as catheters and stomas;
- help with eating and to manage special diets;
- help with applying creams, eye drops or dressings;
- help with getting up and going to bed;
- help with getting dressed;
- help to move about indoors;
- memory and safety devices that help your parent to manage: for example, systems to remind them to take medicines, or sound/movement alarms linked to light controls.

Local councils are allowed to charge for any services that do not come under personal care and each one will have its own charging policy. Your parent's local council should be able to provide you with information explaining how its charges are worked out.

CAN MY PARENTS GET FREE PERSONAL CARE IF I'M ARRANGING IT FOR THEM?

If you are arranging and paying for your parent's personal care, you will need to ask their local council for an assessment (see 'Care assessment', page 18). If the local council agrees that your parent needs personal care services, it can:

- make a contractual arrangement with the agency providing the care, and pay it directly; or
- give your parent the cash to pay the carer or care agency (Direct Payments).

However, the local council may not agree to pay for all of the services your parent is currently receiving. It will contribute towards the cost of care only up to the level it has assessed your parent as needing. It will also have its own rules about the kinds of services it will offer, how much care your parent will be given and how often. You can arrange for your parent to continue to receive other services but you will have to carry on arranging and paying for them yourself.

LIVE-IN HELP

Your parent may wish to have someone live with them full-time to help with chores and their personal care. This offers the advantages of only one person being involved at a time (care agencies providing live-in carers normally change the carer every few weeks) as well as round-the-clock care. Particularly in rural areas, where part-time care may be difficult to find, this can be a good arrangement.

However, it is very expensive and although, following a care assessment (and depending on your parent's financial position), social services may pay a proportion of the costs, the long-term implications should be considered. For example, would other family members be willing to contribute financially if your parent can no longer meet the additional costs? Would emergency care be available if the live-in carer were to fall ill? Nevertheless, if your parent has just come out of hospital and requires a lot of help for a short period of time, someone living with them could be just what they need. Equally for families that are financially secure or for a parent who has a terminal illness and does not wish to leave their own home, live-in care can offer the best solution. Ask social services about agencies that provide live-in carers.

CARE AT HOME AFTER HOSPITAL DISCHARGE

Your parent should be given up to four weeks' free care at home after discharge from hospital. This covers both personal and non-personal care. (See 'Coming out of hospital', page 185.)

CARE SERVICES IN NORTHERN IRELAND

Older people who live in Northern Ireland should not have to pay for any home help services they receive from the local council if they are:

- aged 75 and over; or
- are in receipt of Pension Credit or Income Support.

The home help service includes:

- basic household tasks: for example, cleaning, preparing and cooking food, and shopping; and
- some personal and social care duties: for example, help with washing, dressing, going to the toilet and supervising medicines.

If your parent does not automatically qualify for free home help, the local council will assess your parent's finances to see how much they should contribute. This will include any income from earnings, pensions and most benefits. However, any Attendance Allowance or Disability Living Allowance they receive should be ignored. The value of your parent's home will not be counted, but other savings and capital may be taken into account.

PAYING FOR EQUIPMENT AND ADAPTATIONS

Your parent should not be charged for any community care equipment, but they may be asked to contribute to the cost of adaptations, depending on their financial situation.

WITHDRAWAL OF SERVICES

Local councils can take their resources into account when they are setting the eligibility criteria for their services. They can also, within limits, revise these eligibility criteria for financial reasons: in other words they can reduce or cut the services they offer (see box for advice).

REDUCTION OF SERVICES BY LOCAL COUNCIL

If your parent's local council wishes to withdraw or reduce services being received, the following advice may be of help.

- Before it can withdraw or reduce services, the local council has to reassess the person's needs. This means that it should carry out a full assessment of these needs against its new eligibility criteria.

- This reassessment should involve a personal visit – a letter telling the individual that services are being withdrawn is not enough. If your parent receives a letter from the local council telling them that services are being reduced or cut, you should contact the council, say that you do not accept that your parent has been reassessed, and ask for a personal visit.

- If your parent's services are being threatened, seek advice immediately. It is important that your parent lodges a complaint with the local council as quickly as possible. (See 'Making a complaint', page 22, or call the Help the Aged service SeniorLine.)

LIVING IN SHELTERED ACCOMMODATION

'It tends to be expensive in relation to the market, but the high degree of independence afforded to us makes it worth every penny – not only to us, but also to our children, who feel that we have a very good quality of life and, because none of them live nearby, are reassured that an eye is being kept on us.' *(father)*

'Prospective buyers need to do their research! Try and talk to residents and read the small print of any lease.' *(father)*

'Although we don't live far away, it was a relief when mum moved into her flat. There's a big age range but she's definitely met people she likes.' (*daughter*)

Sheltered housing is specially designed for older residents. It can offer your parents the choice of living independently while still having the security of knowing that, if anything went wrong, help is at hand. For you, especially if you do not live near your parents, it can offer the peace of mind that should one of them fall ill or need help urgently, someone will be available to assist. If the accommodation is chosen wisely, your parents will be in a housing complex where they will feel relaxed and able to make new friends. If they are becoming less mobile and do not or perhaps no longer drive, living in sheltered housing can avoid the stresses of loneliness and isolation that can develop among some older people who stay in their own home.

There are many different types of sheltered housing schemes, but most have a scheme or house manager (or warden) and provide 24-hour emergency assistance through an alarm system. Accommodation is self-contained, but there are usually some areas that everyone can use, such as a common room or lounge. Many schemes run social events for residents. Sheltered housing might appeal to your parents if they want to live independently, perhaps in a smaller and easier-to-manage home, but like the idea of having someone to call on in an emergency.

The role of the scheme manager varies widely, but he or she does not usually provide regular care or help with cooking and housework. If your parents need this sort of help you can help them apply for services such as home care or meals on wheels from social services (social work department in Scotland or health and social services trust in Northern Ireland). The scheme manager may be able to help you to arrange whatever help is needed or suggest whom you should contact.

To cover the costs of running the sheltered housing scheme, residents pay a service charge. The amount residents have to pay will vary, so if your parents are interested in a scheme it is important to ask how much it costs, exactly what the service charge covers, and what it does not include.

If your parents like the idea of sheltered housing, they will need to decide whether to rent or buy. If they own their home at the moment they will probably want to buy – both for the investment and because it can be difficult for home owners to rent from local councils or housing associations. But providers of rented sheltered housing can be flexible and may look at your parents' application sympathetically if they have good reasons for wanting to move. Policies vary widely from area to area; to find out how things work in your parents' area contact their housing department or local housing associations.

RENTING SHELTERED HOUSING

Most sheltered housing for rent is provided by local councils and by housing associations, which are groups that provide housing for people who would not usually be able to afford to buy their own homes.

To find out about local council sheltered housing, contact the housing department at your parents' local council (or their local housing executive in Northern Ireland). If they qualify to apply, they will be sent an application form to fill in. There is often a waiting list for sheltered housing, so ask how long they might have to wait and whether their application will be given priority.

Each local council has its own allocation policy which explains how it decides who gets offered council housing. Many housing departments will give a higher place on the waiting list to someone with health problems, or if their current house is unsuitable in some way. Others will only offer housing to people who have lived in the council's area for a particular length of time.

How long your parents have to wait will often depend on how flexible they are. If they are only prepared to consider one particular area or type of property they will probably have longer to wait than would be the case if they were happy to look at whatever is available. Again, talk to the local housing department so that the staff know what sort of housing your parents are willing to consider.

Housing associations also provide sheltered housing for rent. Many housing associations have an agreement with the local council that they will offer housing to people already on the council's register. Also, in some areas the local council and a number of housing associations operate joint waiting lists. Ask your parents' local council if they work with housing associations in this way.

You may also be able to apply directly to a housing association. To apply, you first need to find out which housing associations provide sheltered housing in your parents' area.

- The local housing department (or housing executive in Northern Ireland) will be able to give you a list of housing association schemes in the area.
- The local Citizens Advice Bureau or housing advice centre should keep a list of local housing associations providing sheltered housing.
- Elderly Accommodation Counsel (EAC) can provide details of housing association schemes in any area you ask for.

Contact each housing association to find out what is available and whether your parents can apply for housing with them. Different housing associations may have different rules for working out to whom they can offer housing.

BUYING SHELTERED HOUSING

Sheltered housing for sale is nearly always built by private developers. For your parents' protection, buy only from a builder who is registered with the National House-Building Council (NHBC), and is covered by its Sheltered Housing Code. Once all the properties have been sold, the scheme is usually run by a separate management group, which employs the scheme manager and organises maintenance and other services. The quality of the service provided by the management company can have a great effect on a scheme; check whether it adheres to a code of practice.

Be sure to get advice from a solicitor, or from a bank or building society, before going ahead with the purchase. It is essential to get expert financial and legal advice, not only on buying the property, but also on the terms of the lease, the service charge and the running costs. Elderly Accommodation Counsel can provide details of private sheltered housing developments in any area you ask for.

PURCHASING SCHEMES

If your parents are home owners and want to move into sheltered accommodation, but know that the money they will get from selling their present home will not cover the cost of buying somewhere new, what can they do?

This is a difficult situation. They could ask about renting sheltered housing (see above), but whether they will be offered accommodation depends very much on the policies of the council or housing associations in their area. There are a few other possibilities you can look into if your parents find themselves in this situation, but it is as well to realise that not all of these options are widely available.

■ Some housing associations run shared-ownership schemes, which involve part-buying and part-renting a property.
■ A few private companies run Life Interest Plans, which allow older people to buy the right to live in a property for the rest of their lives, often for well below the normal market price of the property.

Elderly Accommodation Counsel can tell you whether there are any schemes of this kind in your parents' area, and who runs them. If your parents are thinking about either of these options it is vital for them to get independent legal advice before signing any agreement.

MAKING A DECISION ON SHELTERED HOUSING

Before making the decision to move into sheltered accommodation, be sure to ask about the financial arrangements, how the scheme is set up and whether it will suit your parents (see box).

BUYING A SHELTERED ACCOMMODATION PROPERTY

If your parents are considering this, you and they will want to find out:

- who is responsible for repairs and maintenance, including major items such as lift renewals?
- what happens if your parents want to sell the property later on?
- what happens if one or both of them should become frail and need more care?

BUYING OR RENTING SHELTERED HOUSING

Buyers and renters alike need to ask these questions:

- how is the service charge worked out?
- what is included in this?
- are there plans to change it?
- is there a record of past increases? If the scheme is so new that there is no record of past service charges, ask for records from another scheme that the organisation runs.
- what is the accommodation like?
- is there room for favourite pieces of furniture?
- is there enough storage space?
- what sort of heating is there?
- are pets allowed?
- what is the role of the scheme manager?
- how does the alarm system work?
- is there 24-hour cover?
- what are the communal facilities like? Is there a lounge, a laundry, a guest room for visitors?
- are social events organised, by either residents or the scheme manager?
- is the location convenient for local facilities such as shops, library, doctor's surgery and public transport?

No doubt many other questions will occur to you and your parents; it is a good idea to jot these down and use them as a checklist when visiting the scheme. Talk to the scheme manager and to some of the people who live there to get an idea of how things work, and discuss with your parents whether it is the sort of atmosphere that would suit them. Is it close enough for you to visit frequently? It is essential that you all feel happy and comfortable about where your parents move to, so find out as much as you can before making a decision.

'EXTRA CARE' AND 'CLOSE CARE' SHELTERED HOUSING

Some housing associations, voluntary organisations, local councils and commercial companies offer very sheltered or 'extra care' housing. These schemes provide meals and help with domestic tasks and personal care for people who are less able to manage. 'Close care' housing is usually located in the grounds of a care home, with staff from the home providing extra care and assistance. Elderly Accommodation Counsel can give you details of any schemes of this kind in your parents' area.

Abbeyfield societies are voluntary organisations that run supported sheltered housing in family-style households with 8–12 residents. Supervised by a house manager, the schemes provide two cooked meals a day. Although most Abbeyfield residents are tenants, some societies still use licences: this means that the tenure of residents is less secure. If your parents could be interested in an Abbeyfield scheme, ask if this is the case; and ensure that advice is obtained from a solicitor or Citizens Advice Bureau before a decision to move in is made.

OTHER ACCOMMODATION OPTIONS

There are also some other options to consider. For example, some areas have almshouses. Run by charitable trusts, these provide low-cost accommodation to older people in need. Most almshouses have their own rules as to whom they house. For more information on almshouses in your parents' area, contact Elderly Accommodation Counsel (see chapter 6).

Some councils and housing associations have housing schemes which are specially designed for older people but do not have a scheme manager; these properties are usually conveniently located for shops and services. Similarly, some private developers sell homes which have special design features that make them especially appropriate for older people. This type of accommodation is not classed as sheltered housing because there is no resident scheme manager.

Elderly Accommodation Counsel can provide you with details of this sort of housing in all areas. Your parents' local council and housing associations will also be able to tell you about any schemes that they run.

RESIDENTIAL CARE

'I would rather have a pill to put me to sleep like my cat than go into a nursing home.' (*older woman with no family*)

'I wish my children would take me home sometimes.' (*mother*)

'The food's good here and the people are good too. I enjoy playing bingo.' (*mother*)

'I do feel guilty that my mum's "in a home", but she's wheelchair-bound and knows there's no realistic alternative. She'd obviously prefer to be in her own home, but she's got a lovely room and the staff seem very caring.' (*daughter*)

For some time it has been government policy to encourage older people to continue to live independently in the community. As a result, there are fewer care homes and it can be difficult to have your parent assessed as needing full-time care. However, at some point it may become appropriate for your parent to become resident in a care home and you may need to be assertive when your parent has a Care Assessment if you wish this alternative to be seriously considered.

This may happen after an accident or illness that has left your parent more frail, or perhaps after the death of a spouse who was also the main carer. If you have been your parent's main carer, you will probably find the move into a residential home emotionally painful, almost like bereavement. This is a normal reaction but may be helped by becoming involved with your parent's life in their new environment and having a good relationship with the care-home staff.

Whatever the reason for the move into the care home, even if you think it is for your parent's personal safety and well-being, it is important that they are involved with the decision-making and not made to feel incapable or unloved. After the move, you need to make an effort to ensure that your parent still feels part of the family and that you care about them just as you did before. With busy lives elsewhere, it can be easy to postpone a visit to your parent or delay taking them out for the day, but wherever they live, it will be crucial for your parent's well-being, health and happiness to keep them involved in the lives of all the family as much as possible.

Care homes vary tremendously, and in the same way as if you were moving home yourself, it is only reasonable that you should find somewhere where your parent feels they will be able to settle happily.

TRIAL PERIODS OR RESPITE CARE IN CARE HOMES

A stay in a care home does not have to be permanent. You might want your parent to stay in a care home just for a short period to give them a chance to recover after an illness or to give you, as their carer, a break. Most homes keep beds free for respite care.

If your parent is worried about whether living in a care home is the right choice, you can reassure them that arrangements can be made for them to stay in a home as a temporary resident to see how they get on.

MOVING INTO A CARE HOME

If you and your parent think that a care home is the right choice, the move needs to be seen by all concerned as a positive step. Despite the many fears your parent may have, moving into a care home can be a big relief for people who have been struggling at home or have become isolated. Care homes can offer a secure and comfortable environment as well as the opportunity to be in the company of other people.

If your parent is thinking about moving into a care home, the first step is to contact the local council social services department and ask for an assessment of their needs (see 'Care assessment', page 18). If the local council agrees that they need to move into a care home, they may get help towards the cost of the care home fees.

Once you have asked for an assessment, someone from the social services department should visit your parent to discuss their personal situation. This should include things like their health, how they currently manage at home and what sort of help they need. It is probably a good idea that you or another relative or friend is with your parent when they have the assessment.

It is worth your parent and you making a note of what needs to be discussed in advance. For example, your parent might want to move to a different area to be closer to you or other relatives, or live somewhere where they can keep their pet. The assessment must take into account your parent's own wishes, so make sure that they are not afraid to say what they think.

Once the assessment has taken place, the local council may suggest that the best way to meet your parent's care needs is for them to move into a care home. If this is the case, the local council has a responsibility to arrange and pay for the care – unless your parent is able to do so.

LOCAL AUTHORITY COMPLAINTS PROCEDURE

If you are unhappy with the result of your parent's assessment, or how it was carried out, you can make a complaint. All local councils must have a straightforward complaints procedure; see 'Making a complaint', page 22, and contact the social services department for details. If you need help or advice with making a complaint, the Help the Aged

SeniorLine service or your local Citizens Advice Bureau, or Age Concern may be able to help you.

PAYING FOR A PLACE IN A CARE HOME

The full cost of a care home place can be met by contributions from different sources. If your parent's local council has agreed that they need to move into a care home, it may pay part or all of the fees, depending on how much income and savings your parent has. The council will work out how much your parent should contribute. If your parent is assessed as needing nursing care, the NHS may also make a contribution. In some circumstances all the care fees may be paid by the NHS.

- The financial aspects of moving into a care home can seem complicated, but there are rules for working out how much your parent will pay. To find out more about funding a care home place, contact your parent's local Citizens Advice Bureau or the Help the Aged service SeniorLine.

Local authority funding

If your parent has been assessed as needing to move into a care home, the local council will work out how much needs to be contributed towards the cost. It should explain how the contribution is worked out and what your parent will have to pay. Check that your parent gets this information in writing.

Make sure you and your parent understand exactly what is included in the fees and know what will have to be paid for in addition. For example, will your parent have to use their personal expenses allowance to pay for toiletries, phone calls, outings or clothing? Or are any of these things included in the fees?

If the local council is responsible for funding all or part of the fees, it is responsible for paying the fees directly to the home. If your parent is contributing part of the fees, they will have to refund this amount to the local council.

If the local council decides your parent can pay the full fees, it will probably expect them (or you) to arrange the care home place. If your parent is not able to manage this, and there is no one else local who can help, the local council must arrange a suitable placement.

Giving away property and savings

It is illegal to give property or savings to another person in order to qualify for financial help from your local council. This is called 'deprivation of assets'. If the local authority believes that your parent has deliberately given away assets so as to reduce or avoid fees for accommodation it may try to claim the fees back.

It is important to remember that if your parent gives away their home, they may lose control over what happens to it. Although you may feel that your parent is well protected if they give their home to you or their other children or members of the family, they may have no legal rights if circumstances change. As the majority of older people do not need to move into a care home, you may wish to advise your parent to hold on to their home and capital, and to preserve their independence and control of their own money. If you are concerned about any future deterioration in your parent's health or mental capacities, you should suggest that your parent signs a lasting power of attorney (see page 121).

Nursing care contribution in England and Wales

Before the move into a care home, a Care Assessment should be arranged by the social services department of the local council. If, as a result, the local council thinks that your parent needs nursing care, it should organise for your parent to be assessed by a registered nurse. If, as a result of this assessment, your parent is deemed to be in need of care from a qualified nurse, the NHS should make a contribution towards the care home fees. The NHS would pay an amount directly to the care home. If your parent pays their own care home fees this should mean there is a reduction in how much they have to pay.

If you or your parent disagrees with the decision made by the nurse, a review can be requested.

Fully funded NHS care

If your parent's medical needs are considered to be 'complex or intense or unpredictable' they may get completely free care from the NHS. This is known as continuing NHS health care. Your parent should be assessed for continuing NHS health care before they move into a care home that provides nursing care, or when they are being discharged from hospital. Your parent can also ask for an assessment if they live in a care home that does not provide nursing care.

Unfortunately it can be very difficult to qualify for fully funded NHS care. Each local primary care trust (or health board in Scotland and Wales) has its own set of rules – known as eligibility criteria – for deciding who gets this type of care.

If your parent is informed that they do not meet the criteria for continuing NHS health care, and you are both unhappy with this decision, you can use their complaints procedure. It will help if you get advice first – for example, from your local Citizens Advice Bureau.

If your parent does receive free continuing NHS health care, the choice about where the care is provided is up to the NHS, though they do have to take your parent's views into account.

THE RIGHT TO CHOOSE A HOME

Even if the local council is arranging and paying for the care home, your parent should have some choice as to which home they move to. It should not be a case of your parent having to move to wherever there happens to be a place.

Your parent's local council may suggest a particular home, or offer a choice of homes. However, your parent may not like the suggested home when they visit it, or you and they may have a particular home in mind. If so, you can ask the local council to arrange a place for them in the home that you prefer. If they move to a home outside the local council area, it will still be responsible for arranging payment.

If you choose a home that is in another country in the UK you will need to contact your parent's local council to see if they can make a special arrangement. However, if your parent is in Northern Ireland

and they want to move to England, Scotland or Wales the situation is more complicated. Contact the Help the Aged service SeniorLine (see chapter 6) for more advice.

Apart from the restrictions mentioned above, your parent should be able to move to the home of their choice as long as:

- the chosen home has a place available;
- it is suitable for your parent's assessed needs;
- the home will enter into a contract with the local council under the council's usual conditions; and
- it does not cost any more than the local council would usually expect to pay for someone with your parent's needs.

TOP-UP FEES

You may want your parent to move to a home that costs more than the authority would normally pay. In this case, someone else (usually a relative or a charity) may make up the difference. However, if this is an option for your parent, check what will happen if the fees go up in the future. Will the third party be able to meet the additional costs? Will the local council have a responsibility to cover part of the increased fees?

Your parent cannot usually top up their own fees. In England, Scotland and Wales they can do this only if:

- they have a deferred payment agreement with the local council; or
- their property is being disregarded for the first 12 weeks of entering into care.

In Northern Ireland your parent cannot top up their own fees; they can only get help from a third party. However, this may change, so check with SeniorLine (see chapter 6).

MOVING INTO A CARE HOME FROM HOSPITAL
(See 'Coming out of hospital', page 185.)

If your elderly parent has been in hospital following an accident or illness, they will probably have a Care Assessment before being discharged. It may involve seeing how your parent manages a staircase unaided and whether they are capable of looking after their personal needs and can make a cup of tea or something to eat. The assessment is carried out to decide if additional help is required for them to return to their own home or whether their needs can best be met in a care home. The hospital staff should contact social services and make arrangements if your parent will need ongoing help but it is always worth checking with the ward personnel that this has been done.

ARRANGING AND PAYING FOR YOUR PARENT'S OWN CARE HOME PLACE

If your parent can afford to pay for their own place in a home, you do not have to go through the local council. You can approach the home your parent would like to live in directly and sort out the financial arrangements yourselves.

However, if there is any chance at all that your parent might need help with fees in the future, it is strongly recommended that your parent has their care needs assessed by the local council before you make any private arrangements.

This is because a time may come when your parent cannot afford to pay the fees. If you then ask the local council to assess your parent, their needs assessment might not include paying for the home of your parent's choice. It also needs to be recognised that care requirements may change and although your parent may need relatively little help with personal care at the moment, in future they may develop more complex needs.

If you do decide to make your own arrangements, Relatives and Residents Association produces a useful 'framework contract' for people arranging their own care.

If your parent has some capital you may want advice on the best way of investing it to pay for future care. The Care Fees Advice service run by Help the Aged is designed to help older people plan their finances to meet any future care costs. Alternatively, your parent may want to talk to their own solicitor or financial adviser.

FINDING A CARE HOME

Your parent has a right to choose which home they move into. So you will probably want to find out what homes there are in your parent's area and visit a few together to get an idea of what they are like.

As a first step, try asking around: perhaps friends or relatives know of a home with a good reputation. But remember, although a personal recommendation is a good starting point, homes can change, and what suits one person may not suit another.

WHO ARE CARE HOMES RUN BY?

Care homes can be run directly by local councils; by voluntary organisations (registered charities or religious bodies); or privately (by individuals or companies on a commercial basis).

Homes run by voluntary organisations may have special rules about whom they can admit. For example, some homes are for people who have served in the armed forces, or for people from particular ethnic groups or religions.

CARE HOMES WITHIN A SPECIFIC AREA

There are different ways of finding out about care homes in your preferred area:

- contact the local care standards authority: it can give you information about the homes registered in the locality;
- in Northern Ireland, contact the local health and social services trust for registered homes in the locality;
- the charity Counsel and Care provides information and advice on finding a home and what to look for;
- Elderly Accommodation Counsel (EAC) has a comprehensive database of care homes in the UK. It focuses on aspects directly related to quality of life within the care home setting.

WHO REGULATES CARE HOMES?

Care homes are registered and regulated by the following care standards authorities:

- the Commission for Social Care Inspection in England;
- the Care and Social Services Inspectorate for Wales in Wales;
- the Scottish Commission for the Regulation of Care in Scotland; and
- the Regulation and Quality Improvement Authority in Northern Ireland.

Since April 2006 care homes must be inspected at least once every three years, although they can be inspected more often if it is felt necessary. After each inspection an 'inspection report' is produced, containing information about how the care home operates. You should be able to get copies of these reports from your care standards authority (or health and social services board in Northern Ireland). See chapter 6 for details.

WHAT KIND OF RESIDENTIAL CARE IS NEEDED?

Care homes have to be very clear what level of care they provide and how they will meet each resident's care needs.

All care homes should be able to give help with personal care if it is required: this could include help with washing, dressing and going to the toilet.

If your parent is extremely frail or bedridden, or has any sort of medical condition or illness that means they need a lot of attention from a doctor or nurse, they will probably need to look for a care home that can provide nursing care. This type of home should have a qualified nurse on duty 24 hours a day.

Finding a home for someone with very specific care needs – for example, someone with severe dementia – can sometimes be difficult. If you cannot find a home that provides the sort of care your parent needs, ask your local council to help; it has a responsibility to find a suitable home for anyone it has assessed as needing a care home place.

The Alzheimer's Society can advise on suitable homes for someone with dementia. Other specialist groups, such as the Stroke Association or the Parkinson's Disease Society, can offer specialist advice and guidance.

WHAT TO LOOK FOR IN A HOME

Care homes vary a good deal with regard to type of building, location and general atmosphere, but they all have to abide by care standards which cover key aspects of living in a care home. These standards include rights to privacy and dignity, how staff handle medicines, heating and lighting levels and handling residents' money.

Your library should have a copy of these minimum care standards or ask one of the care homes that you are interested in for a copy. If your parent lives in Northern Ireland, contact the Northern Ireland Regulation and Quality Improvement Authority to find out about care standards.

NARROWING THE SEARCH FOR A CARE HOME

Once you have found out about homes in your parent's area, get in touch with a few and ask them to send you a brochure. Give the brochures to your parent to look through at their leisure and arrange to visit those that appeal so that you can both get an idea of what is available. You might want to take another member of your family or one of your parent's friends, too, for another opinion.

If you have been your parent's primary carer until this time, this will be a doubly difficult and sensitive task to deal with. You may be more than aware that your parent's needs have become too great for you to handle adequately at home, but, at the same time, you may have feelings of guilt and sadness. Your parent may also be feeling vulnerable and display signs of displeasure. Nevertheless, it is a good idea to visit as many homes as appear to suit your parent's needs.

If it is impossible for you both to get to all the various homes, ask if someone from the home can come to you. You and your parent can then ask questions and get some idea of what the home is like.

You could also visit some of the homes with another family member or friend and make sure that you ask the questions that would be of greatest concern to your parent. You can take digital photographs and show them to your parent when you return.

When you visit a care home there will be many things you might want to look out for and ask about. Make a list before you go of things you and your parent want to know. If your parent has strong religious beliefs you might want to ensure that the home will accommodate these, or to find a home which is run by people who share those beliefs.

Do not be embarrassed about asking lots of questions. It is sensible to do as much research as you can when you are making such a major decision about someone's future. If you can, speak to people who already live in the home, encourage your parent to sit and chat with them so that they can get an idea of what it is really like to live there. After you have visited a few different care homes, you will start to get a feeling of a place's atmosphere almost as soon as you walk into one.

Everyone has different ideas about what they want from where they live. What is especially important to your parent? The box suggests examples of questions that you might want to ask and things to look out for.

CARE HOME STAFF

You will find it useful to watch how staff behave. Are they always rushing around or do they spend time talking to individual residents? Are people encouraged to do what they can for themselves, or do staff take over? Are members of staff friendly and helpful? Do they treat the residents in an appropriate adult manner or more like children?

CARE HOME MEALS

Is there a choice of meals and can your parent choose when and where to eat? Does the home cater for special diets? Is there variety in the menus? Are the meals nutritious and are the servings generous? Are there facilities for your parent to make a snack as and when they want?

THE CARE HOME/RESIDENT CONTRACT

In much the same way as if you were choosing sheltered housing for your parent, when choosing a care home you need to make sure you know exactly where you stand.

- Will there be a written contract between your parent and the home?
- What exactly will the fees cover and what extras will you be expected to pay for? For example, will your parent have to provide their own toiletries, or continence pads?
- Will your parent's room in the home be secure? Could you be asked to find them alternative accommodation at short notice?
- In the event of the home having to close, or be transferred to another provider, how would the home ensure that your parent's interests are a priority?
- How does the home handle problems and complaints?
- Is there a residents' committee and a relatives' group?
- What would happen if your parent fell ill and needed more care? Would they have to move?
- Is there a policy on smoking?

CARE HOME LOCATION

Does your parent like to visit the shops, social club, library, park or any other places? If so, you will want to ensure that the home you choose is within walking distance or that transport is available.

CARE HOME POLICY ON PETS

Your parent may have a pet that they wish to bring with them: will this be possible? If not, do they allow people to bring animals into the home when they visit? Elderly Accommodation Counsel keeps details of homes that allow pets. If this turns out to be difficult, the Cinnamon Trust can help to re-home your parent's pet if they are unable to take it with them.

VISITORS TO THE CARE HOME

Are there set 'visiting times' or are visitors welcome any time? Is there anywhere for visitors to stay overnight? Are children welcome?

CARE HOME ATMOSPHERE

You and your parent will often be able to get an idea of how well a home is run just by your first impressions. Does it smell clean and fresh? Is there a homely feel or does it seem formal and institutional? Do you like the decoration? Do people seem alert and occupied or are they just dozing in chairs with the TV on in the background? Discuss your feelings after the visit and find out what your parent thinks.

ACTIVITIES IN THE CARE HOME

A good home will provide a range of activities and is likely to have a particular member of staff responsible for organising events for residents. It might have visitors that come in to arrange activities or it might organise day trips. If your parent has a particular interest make sure the home you choose will provide for this, or maybe you can help set something up with other relatives. If your parent enjoys gardening you might want to choose a home with a garden. Age Concern, Counsel and Care and the National Association for the Providers of Activities for Older People (NAPA) can all provide information on arranging activities in care homes. See chapter 6 for details.

YOUR PARENT'S ROOM IN THE CARE HOME

Will your parent have their own bathroom or will they have to share? They may wish to be able to entertain visitors in their own room: can they have their own kettle or tea-making facilities? Can they have a phone in their room or is there a private room where they can make and receive phone calls? Can they bring their own furniture? Will your parent be able to make their own decisions about what time they want to get up and go to bed?

CARE HOME FACILITIES

It is essential to make sure that the home you choose can meet all your parent's care needs. If they have been assessed as needing care in a home by the local authority you may want to take a copy of the assessment with you when you visit the home, so that staff understand what sort of help your parent will need. If they have any particular needs and require special equipment such as bath aids, a special bed, a stair lift or wheelchair access, check that these will be available.

INSPECTION REPORTS

Before making a final decision on a home, you may want to look at a recent inspection report. These often contain a lot of information about how the home operates. For copies of inspection reports, contact the manager of the care home or the care standards authority for your country.

LIVING IN A CARE HOME

Once your parent has moved into a care home, it can take a while for them to settle in. A big change like this can take quite a lot of getting used to and this should be discussed between you beforehand. You too will feel despondent, having to come to terms with the fact that your parent can no longer live independently in the community, and perhaps the thought that entering a care home is one step nearer the end of life.

If you are worried about anything in particular, or are not sure about any aspect of life in your parent's new home, do try to talk to a member of staff about your concerns. Getting any sort of problem out into the open is usually the best way of solving it. Involve your parent in the exercise and ensure that staff knows that you are only trying to make sure that your parent is happily settled. A good manager will recognise that supportive relatives who are keen to be actively involved usually help to maintain a happy atmosphere in the home.

If you would like to talk to someone about what your parent should be able to expect from a care home, or how best to tackle any problems you encounter, contact the Relatives and Residents Association.

The Relatives and Residents Association is a charity set up to support care home residents and their relatives. It operates a telephone helpline and has a network of local groups. See chapter 6 for more details.

You should also refer to the national care standards for care homes for details of the rights of care home residents. The home your parent is in should provide you with a copy.

If you cannot resolve a problem informally, you may wish to make a formal complaint to your parent's home, and also to the body which registers and inspects it. Contact the inspection unit at your care standards authority. Your local Citizens Advice Bureau or Age Concern group might be able to support you in making a complaint of this kind.

You will need to know how to tackle any problems your parent may encounter. But it is equally important to remember that life in a care home can have positive aspects as well. Care homes can provide a safe environment where your parent should get the care and support they need. You may find that your parent soon forms new friendships; and in a good care home they may have the opportunity to enjoy new interests and activities. As always, they will remain a key member of your family and should continue to feel loved and valued.

LIVING WITH YOU

'At her request, I moved in with my daughter and her partner 19 years ago, for what I thought would be my last few years.' (*father*)

'It's emotional stress rather than physical but I would have felt very guilty if I hadn't made an effort and said, "Right — you'll have to go into a home."' (*daughter*)

'I make sure that I pay my way and my daughter says she loves having me. But I still feel in the way. It's like they'll give me a cup of tea, but not include me in their conversation.' (*mother*)

According to research carried out by the Policy Institute, it is usually at a time of crisis (following an illness or accident) that the decision to have an elderly parent move in with an adult child is taken. As a result, there is little time to consider the implications of the decision on all of the family .

Usually, it is an adult daughter who will accommodate a frail parent. and given that women generally live longer than men, the parent is more often than not the mother. It is estimated that one in ten women over 80 who live in private households live with a daughter or son. The typical elderly parent in the Policy Institute study was frail, with poor health, limited mobility and some degree of confusion. Previously they had lived in their own home with help from family and community services, but had decided that they could no longer manage to live alone. Both the parents and the children were unhappy with the prospect of moving to a care home. To a large degree, the daughter or son thought it was their duty to offer their parent a home and the parent, duly grateful, felt indebted to their offspring.

When your parent becomes frailer, the decision to have them to live with you may suit your family. However, once the decision has been made it can be very difficult to change your mind. For a parent who has previously lived independently, this can also be a tremendously difficult transition and they too may regret it. Even if you both agree that you were happier living apart, once you are providing such comprehensive support to your parent, social services may provide some addition care or respite but with limited resources will probably be reluctant to offer a care home alternative.

COMING TO A DECISION ABOUT A MOVE TO YOUR HOME

Perhaps the most important question to ask yourself is how well you and your family get on with your parent while living apart. If you annoy each other now, the chances are that the relationship will be considerably more difficult if you live together.

Think long and hard, consider the points in the box and anything else you can think of. Discuss them with your parent.

BEFORE YOUR PARENT MOVES IN ...

- How will the living arrangements work?
- Will your parent just have a bedroom, or will they have a self-contained bed-sit or even a 'granny flat'?
- Is the house suitable or does it need adaptations?
- Could you get a grant towards adaptations? Contact the local council to find out.
- Could you cope with the physical tasks of caring for your parent? What about any intimate care that they may need?
- How would you deal with the emotional stress?
- What are your partner's thoughts on the matter?
- How will your children manage, particularly if their grandparent becomes increasingly frail and dependent?
- Will you be able to carry on working?
- Will you become a full-time carer?
- Can the responsibility be shared to some degree with your siblings?
- How much privacy will there be for you, your family and your parent?
- Will your parent be able to keep up their own interests and entertain visitors?
- Will your parent share all meals with your family or would you prefer them to be able to cook for themselves sometimes?
- If you have young or teenage children, will your parent find it difficult if there is more noise or mess than they are used to?
- How will the financial and legal arrangements be sorted?
- Will your parent pay rent and help with household bills?

Although it might seem excessive, it is a good idea to have a legal agreement drawn up between you and your parent. This should clarify issues such as who owns the house, what each party is responsible for and what happens if one or other of you ends the arrangement.

It is essential to get legal advice if your parent is selling their current home and/or putting money towards buying a house with your family. Although it might seem awkward or untrusting to seek independent advice, it is better for everyone in the long term that you are all sure of your position before committing yourselves. If you have siblings, involve them. Even if you think you are only doing your duty, they may feel excluded or worried about any future inheritance.

You also need to consider what would happen if your parent's health deteriorated considerably, either mentally or physically. Although we may all hope that our parent will die peacefully in their sleep after a short illness, progressive dementia can put an appalling stress on carers. (See section on common illnesses and disorders, pages 141–80.)

THE RIGHT CHOICE FOR YOUR FAMILY

There is a common misconception that all care homes are inadequate and many adult children feel guilty about the idea of their parents 'going into a home'. Equally, you may know that your parent would be strongly opposed to or even fearful of moving into a home. However, even if you do not want to discuss the option with your parent, if you are worried that having your parent live with you would put undue strain on you and your family, you should at least visit some of the care homes in your area. You may be pleasantly surprised.

If you own your home, or perhaps your children are grown up and you have plenty of space, having your ageing parent live with you may be the right choice for your family. The study from the Policy Institute indicates that if you have an affectionate relationship with your parent and a supportive partner, this will make for a happier household.

Let your parent help financially as much as they want. It can be important to a person's dignity to feel that they are 'paying their way'. No matter what you do, it is almost certain that your parent will feel a burden to some extent, and if they can contribute financially it will make them feel better even if you do not need their money.

From the beginning, encourage your parent to do as much for themselves and around the home as they can. It will make them feel more worthy as well as helping to maintain a level of fitness and independence. Work out a suitable daily routine in order that your parent still feels that they have control over their life. Remember that even if your parent has become less mobile, their mind may still be clear: they do not just need to be lodged and fed, they also need conversation and involvement in the household.

Over time, your parent will probably require more care and, bit by bit, you will discover that you are doing much more for them. This is when you must involve social services to ensure that you get the help you need. If your parent has not had a Care Assessment, arrange one and make sure that you are informed about what services are available and how they will be paid. It is one thing to share your home with your parent but you must still consider your own needs and those of your family. If you get worn down and depressed, you will be of little use to your parent, the rest of your family or yourself.

If you need a break, nag social services for a period of respite care for your parent. It may be possible to provide this in your own home while you go on holiday, or in a care home. Be positive when discussing it with your parent: it can be viewed as a holiday for them too. But whatever your parent's attitude, be resolute if you need a break.

Most families find caring for a parent a manageable but very demanding household arrangement. This needs to be recognised by everyone involved. If you arrive at a stage where your parent is suffering from chronic incontinence or dementia, you should not feel guilty if you can no longer cope. Get help. ■

MONEY AND
MONEY MATTERS

MONEY AND LEGAL MATTERS

When you take responsibility for another person's life, you need to think not just about their physical and emotional well-being but about their finances and the legal issues that become particularly relevant later in life.

PENSIONS

STATE RETIREMENT PENSION

'I don't know what my father receives in pensions and I couldn't ask. He'd never discuss it – it's too personal.' (*daughter*)

'While there's two of us we manage, but problems might arise if only one of us had to run the house.' (*mother*)

'My pension is sufficient for my needs. In fact, I've never been so well-off, but I could not find the money to pay for a place in the sort of care home that I would choose to live in.' (*father*)

About four months before your parent reaches state retirement age (currently 60 for women, though this will gradually rise to 65 from 2010, and 65 for men), they should get a letter inviting them to make a claim for the State Retirement Pension. (The Government intends to equalise the state retirement age at 65 for both men and women. As this change will not start to be phased in until 2010, women born before April 1950 will not be affected.)

The state pension is not paid automatically: your parent will need to make a claim. The claim form is called BR1 and once your parent has filled it in and sent it to the address indicated, their pension entitlement will be calculated. Your parent's pension may be made up of a combination of different types of pension or additions and they will qualify for these in different ways. They may get some of them or all of them.

BASIC PENSION

How much of this basic pension your parent gets depends on how many 'qualifying years' their National Insurance contribution record contains. A qualifying year is a tax year in which they have paid enough contributions towards a pension. They will get a full basic pension if they have a full record.

As a rough guide, your parent should qualify for a full basic pension if they have qualifying years for about 90 per cent of their 'working life' – approximately 44 years for a man and 39 years for a woman. In due course this will be reduced to 30 years for both men and women for those who reach state retirement age on or after 6 April 2010.

If your parent has not paid enough NI contributions to get a full basic pension, they may be able to get a reduced one. In order to get any pension at all they usually need to have qualifying years for at least a quarter of their working life.

People who were unable to work because they were caring for a child or were sick or disabled can reduce the amount of years in their working life which have to be qualifying years.

ADDITIONAL PENSION

Additional pension is extra pension based on the amount your parent earned (and therefore the amount of NI contributions they have made) since April 1978. It is paid under the State Earnings-Related Pension Scheme (SERPS) or through the State Second Pension rules. Your parent does not have to be receiving a basic pension to be entitled to an additional pension. If your parent has been a member of a contracted-out occupational pension scheme or a personal pension scheme, their additional pension will be reduced. A contracted-out deduction will have been made because they will have paid less NI contributions.

GRADUATED PENSION

Graduated Retirement Benefit, or graduated pension, is worked out according to the amount of graduated NI contributions your parent paid between April 1961 and April 1975 (the period when this scheme was running). Your parent may be entitled to graduated pension even if they do not receive a basic or additional pension.

OVER-80S PENSION AND AGE-RELATED ADDITION

The over-80s pension is non-contributory: i.e. people do not have to have made NI contributions in order to receive it. If your parent is 80 or over and gets no basic pension at all they should receive the full amount of over-80s pension. Your parent can apply for the over-80s pension in the four months leading up to their 80th birthday.

When your parent turns 80 they will receive an age-related addition of 25p a week on top of the State Retirement Pension.

INVALIDITY ADDITION

Your parent will get this extra payment on top of whatever pension they are entitled to if they were receiving an invalidity allowance or an age addition with long-term Incapacity Benefit at any time during the eight weeks before they reached pension age. However, the amount they receive will be reduced if they are getting any additional pension.

EXTRA PENSION

Your parent can get an extra amount added to their pension each week if they defer claiming it for at least five weeks

PENSION INCREASES FOR DEPENDANTS

If your parent receives some basic pension, they may be able to get extra pension if their husband, wife or civil partner is dependent on them. The amount they get will depend on how much basic pension they are entitled to.

This will be explained in a letter they will receive after they have made their claim. When the pension payments arrive, they will normally be paid directly into their bank account. If they prefer, they can ask for a cheque to be sent which can be cashed at the post office, but they will then have to rely on the post for the cheque to arrive. If your parent is unable to get to a post office, bank or building society to take out their money, they can arrange for you or someone else to take it out on their behalf. They would need to ask at the post office, bank or building society what arrangements can be made for this.

An additional small tax-free bonus is paid out automatically with the State Retirement Pension shortly before Christmas each year.

STATE RETIREMENT PENSIONS FOR MARRIED WOMEN

Your mother may be entitled to a basic pension in her own right when she reaches the age of 60, because of the NI contributions she built up during her working life.

If she is not entitled to a State Retirement Pension on reaching the age of 60 (perhaps because she did not do any paid work) she may be able to get a basic pension based on her husband's NI contributions. This is called the Married Woman's Pension.

Your mother cannot claim Married Woman's Pension unless her husband is drawing his pension. If your mother is over 60 and her husband has not yet reached 65, her entitlement to any retirement pension will depend on her own contribution record.

WIDOWS

If your mother's husband died before she reached 60 and she has not remarried, she has three main choices when she reaches state retirement age. She should seek advice on which option would be best for her before making a decision.

- She can draw her State Retirement Pension, which can be based on her NI contributions, her late husband's contributions or a combination of both.
- If she was widowed before April 2001 and receives Widow's Pension, she can either continue to receive this until she reaches the age of 65, or she can claim her State

Retirement Pension. The basic amounts will often be the same. If she receives Widow's Pension, she will lose it if she re-marries.

- If she was widowed after April 2001 and is receiving Bereavement Allowance, she can continue to get this until she has been on it for 52 weeks. Alternatively, she can claim her State Retirement Pension as soon as she reaches pension age.

If your mother was widowed after the age of 60 and is not entitled to a pension in her own right, she should be able to get a Retirement Pension based on her late husband's contributions. If she receives some pension, but not the full basic pension, she may also be able to use his NI contribution record to bring her basic pension up to a higher level. She will continue to receive this pension even if she decides to re-marry.

If your parent cannot get any State Retirement Pension, or if the amount they receive is small and they have a low income, they may be entitled to other welfare benefits to help them make ends meet. They can get advice from the Help the Aged SeniorLine service (see chapter 6).

Your parent can draw their State Retirement Pension when they reach pension age even if they are still earning. Their earnings will not affect the amount of pension they receive, but their pension will be counted as part of their taxable income.

DRAWING A PENSION ABROAD

State Retirement Pension will still be paid to your parent if they decide to go to live abroad. However, when pensions rise in the UK they will not automatically receive the increased rate if they are living overseas.

- If they are living in a European Economic Area (EEA) country, or in one of the non-EC countries which has an agreement with the UK, they will receive an uprated pension.

- However, if they are living in a country which has no special arrangement with the UK, their pension will stay frozen at the rate it was when they moved abroad.

Your parent can contact the International Pension Centre at the DWP (see chapter 6) for advice about benefits abroad.

PENSION CREDIT AND OTHER BENEFITS

'Mum and Dad only manage so well because my brothers and I pay the management fees on their retirement flat.' (*daughter*)

'The application forms for help are enormous and it seems that most applications are refused as a matter of course.' (*father*)

Between £2.9 billion and £4.3 billion is left unclaimed by people aged 60 or more. This money is to help with day-to-day expenses, Council Tax, housing costs and health care, but at least 2 million people over 60 fail to claim it each year. Every year more people can claim these benefits. So even if your parent has not been able to get extra money before, they may be able to get help now.

PENSION CREDIT

Pension Credit tops up your parent's weekly income to a basic level that the Government considers necessary. About one-and-a-half million people who could claim Pension Credit do not.

Pension Credit is paid in two parts: **guarantee credit** and **savings credit.** Your parent must be aged at least 60 to get guarantee credit and at 65 they may be able to get savings credit as well. For couples, it is the age of the older partner that counts. Pension Credit rates go up each year by more than State Retirement Pension rates. So even if your parent's income was too high to get any Pension Credit last year, this year it may not be. Even if they have a pension from a job they previously held or some savings, they may still be able to get Pension Credit.

GUARANTEE CREDIT (FOR THOSE AGED 60 OR OVER)

If your parent is aged 60 or more they should qualify for the **guarantee credit** part of Pension Credit if their weekly income is very low. Guarantee credit would bring their income up to a minimum level.

SAVINGS CREDIT (FOR THOSE AGED 65 OR OVER)

If your parent is 65 or more they may get the **savings credit** part of Pension Credit. Savings credit is extra money each week for people who have an income that is higher than the basic State Retirement Pension or have modest savings. Your parent may get it by itself if their income is too high to get guarantee credit. Or they may get some savings credit paid on top of guarantee credit. If your parent is living in partnership with someone, only one partner has to be aged 65 or more.

HOW TO CLAIM PENSION CREDIT

The easiest way to claim Pension Credit is for your parent to make a phone call. They do not need to fill in a form or visit an office. They should just ring a free number (see under 'Pension Credit claims' in chapter 6) and the form will be filled in on their behalf and posted to their home. All they then need to do is check it, sign it and post it back. When your parent calls, it will help if they have their National Insurance number and details of their income and savings to hand.

If your parent needs someone to visit to help with claiming, this can be requested by telephone (for the number, see 'Pension Credit claims' in chapter 6). If they prefer, they can go to the Pension Service website, fill in the form online, print it out and post it.

When your parent sends back the form make sure they send any other documents they are asked for. Make sure that you or they keep a photocopy of everything that has been sent with the date sent written down, in case of any query later. Once the application has been made, the Pension Credit is backdated for up to 12 months. If your parent can get Pension Credit they can also make another claim to get a big reduction in their Council Tax (or rates in Northern Ireland). If your parent is eligible to get the guarantee credit part of Pension Credit they will normally get the whole lot paid. They will also get some or all of their rent paid. They can fill in the claim form over the phone at the same time as they claim Pension Credit.

They may also be able to get free dental treatment, help with the cost of glasses and help with some other expenses. An extra £8.50 a week may be paid, too, for each complete week when the temperature is freezing or below (see page 111 under 'Extra money in winter').

If you are not sure whether or not your parent will be eligible for Pension Credit you can contact the Help the Aged SeniorLine service (see chapter 6) for advice, or encourage your parent to apply anyway. You can also check entitlements to Pension Credit online at www.thepensionservice.gov.uk or at www.entitledto.co.uk.

COUNCIL TAX BENEFIT

About 2 million people aged 60 or more could pay less Council Tax but do not claim: your parent could be one of them.

Council Tax Benefit is paid by reducing the amount of Council Tax due. More people than ever can claim because of recent changes to the system. So even if your parent has applied before but did not qualify, it is worth applying again. If they get the guarantee credit part of Pension Credit they will get all their Council Tax paid, though they will still have to put in a claim. But many people who do not get guarantee credit can also get their Council Tax reduced or paid in full.

How to claim Council Tax Benefit

You or your parent should contact the local authority and ask about Council Tax reductions and Council Tax Benefit. The place to go is the local authority office that sends your parent their Council Tax bill. There should be someone there to help them to fill the form in.

Council Tax Benefit can be backdated for up to 12 months for people over 60. If your parent claims Pension Credit they should be asked to claim Council Tax Benefit at the same time. As mentioned above, the Pension Service will fill in the form for them and send it to them to sign and return to the local council. If your parent already gets Pension Credit they can call the Pension Credit helpline (see chapter 6) for a Council Tax Benefit claim form – a simple, three-page one. If you or your parent have internet access you can check your parent's entitlement to Council Tax Benefit at www.entitledto.co.uk.

More help with Council Tax

A special Council Tax Benefit can be paid in some cases even if income or savings are too high to get the normal Council Tax Benefit. Your parent can get it if they are single (or not living with their spouse) and has someone living in their home who meets all the following conditions:

- is aged 18 or over
- is not paying your parent rent
- is not your parent's husband, wife or civil partner
- is not living with your parent as a couple
- does not have to pay Council Tax themselves
- has a low income.

This reduction is called Alternative Maximum Council Tax Benefit and it is claimed by less than one person in ten who could get it. If your parent qualifies for normal Council Tax Benefit and for Alternative Maximum Council Tax Benefit, they cannot get them both. They will get whichever is higher.

HOUSING BENEFIT

Up to 380,000 people over 60 could get help with their rent but do not claim. Some of them could get all their rent paid. Could one of them could be your parent?

If your parent is a tenant they may be able to get help with their rent through Housing Benefit. If they are a council or housing association tenant, Housing Benefit is paid by reducing the amount of rent they have to pay. If they are a private tenant, Housing Benefit is normally paid directly into their bank account or by cheque; the tenant pays the landlord in the normal way. Some older people can get all their rent paid – including those who get the guarantee credit part of Pension Credit.

It is simple to find out whether your parent should be getting Housing Benefit. Your parent needs to contact the local council and ask about help to pay their rent. It can be backdated for up to one year for people over 60. If they claim Pension Credit and they pay rent, they should be asked to claim Housing Benefit at the same time. The Pension Service will fill in the form and send it to your parent to sign and return to the local council.

If you or your parent have internet access you can also check their entitlement to Housing Benefit at www.entitledto.co.uk.

DISCRETIONARY HOUSING PAYMENTS

Even if your parent gets Housing Benefit or Council Tax Benefit they may not be able to meet their housing costs. If so, they can apply for extra money called a Discretionary Housing Payment which can help with rent or Council Tax. Each local council has its own budget and rules. If your parent is too embarrassed to ask for help, you can contact their local council on their behalf about how they can apply for extra money.

RATES IN NORTHERN IRELAND

The rating system in Northern Ireland changed on 1 April 2007. Rates on property are now based on its capital value at 1 January 2005. Any householder should have been informed of the value during 2006. If your parent thinks the valuation is wrong they should make a formal application for a review to the District Valuer. If necessary, they can then appeal further. Full details are available on www.vla.nics.gov.uk or from the district office of the Valuation and Lands Agency (see chapter 6). Your parent can call this office for more help.

If the rates bill for your parent's property has increased by more than a third, they will automatically get transitional relief – which means they do not have to apply for help. The bill will have risen by a third in 2007/8 and then the extra will be phased in over the following two years. The full rates will be payable in 2010/11.

If your parent is disabled and their property has been modified because of their disability then they are entitled to a Disabled Person's Allowance of 25 per cent off the rates. If your parent already has an allowance of more than that, they will be allowed to keep it.

HELP WITH OTHER EXPENSES

FUNERAL PAYMENT

If your parent's husband, wife or civil partner dies, they may get help with the cost of their funeral if they are receiving Council Tax Benefit, Housing Benefit, Pension Credit or Working Tax Credit with a disability addition.

If perhaps a brother or sister dies and your parent is the closest relative, they may get help with the cost of the funeral if they are getting one of the above benefits. However, if there is another relative with a similar connection (for example, another brother or sister) and who is not getting a means-tested benefit, they will be expected to pay.

The payment will cover a burial plot and the burial or cremation fee – though not the cost of burying ashes – and any associated medical expenses. Your parent will get up to £700 to cover most of the rest of the costs of the funeral. If the deceased had a funeral payment plan, up to £120 can still be claimed for these costs if they are not covered by the plan. In addition, your parent can apply for the cost of one return journey within the UK to make the arrangements, and, if the body must be moved more than 80 kilometres (about 50 miles) within the UK, the extra costs of bringing the body home will also be covered. Your parent must claim within three months of the funeral, on a form available from your parent's local benefits office.

Note that the Funeral Payment may be reclaimed by the Department for Work and Pensions from any cash available from the deceased person's estate.

SOCIAL FUND PAYMENTS

People who get Pension Credit (guarantee credit, savings credit or both) may be able to get help with some extra expenses from the Social Fund. The Fund is different from other benefits.

Different offices apply the rules differently so it is important to seek advice from your parent's local Citizens Advice Bureau or other advice agency before making an application.

COMMUNITY CARE GRANTS

If your parent is finding it hard to manage at home because of age or illness and is receiving Pension Credit, they may get a Community Care Grant. The grant can cover the cost of moving to accommodation which is more suitable to their needs or which is nearer to relatives who will help to look after them. It can also pay essential expenses to help your parent stay where they are rather than go into a care home or hospital. If your parent is already in a care home or hospital, they may get a grant to help them move out into their own accommodation.

A Community Care Grant can pay for minor essential repairs which are your parent's responsibility and the cost of reconnecting fuel supplies. It can pay for heaters, bedding and help with laundry costs, including a washing machine in some cases. It can also pay for special or essential items of furniture or equipment.

Your parent will only get the full grant if they have less than £1,000 savings. They will be expected to use anything over £1,000 towards paying for what they need.

TRAVELLING EXPENSES

If your parent is receiving Pension Credit and he has a close relative who is ill, they may get a Community Care Grant to pay for the cost of visiting them in a hospital or care home, or even in their own home. Your parent may possibly get a grant to visit a friend or more distant relative. They may also get a grant to attend a relative's funeral. Your parent would normally get their fare on standard-class public transport and money for essential overnight stops. However, they will only get the full amount if they have less than £1,000 savings. If they expect to be visiting someone regularly, they should ask for a grant to cover visits for up to six months.

BUDGETING LOANS

If your parent has been getting any Pension Credit for at least six months, they may get a Budgeting Loan of between £100 to £1,500 to help pay for essential and expensive items. These loans have to be paid back out of their weekly Pension Credit and your parent cannot get one if they have savings of more than £2,000. Budgeting Loans can result in more debt and difficulty. It is always better to try to get a grant.

HOW TO CLAIM A SOCIAL FUND PAYMENT

Your parent can apply for a Community Care Grant or a Budgeting Loan on a form available from the local Jobcentre Plus office. If you live far away and are unable to help your parent, one of the staff should help them to fill it out.

Even if your parent meets all the conditions to get a Social Fund grant or loan, they may find that they are refused. Each area has only a fixed amount of money for the payments and it is possible that they will not have enough to meet all the claims.

EXTRA MONEY IN WINTER

If your parent gets any Pension Credit, they will get an extra payment each complete week that the weather is very cold. This Cold Weather Payment is £8.50 a week and is made for any period of seven days when the temperature is freezing or below, or it is forecast to be that cold. This payment will be sent automatically – it does not have to be claimed.

Every household that includes someone aged 60 or more will get a Winter Fuel Payment to help with their fuel bills. The payment is £200 if there is someone aged at least 60 in the house and £300 if there is someone aged at least 80. The qualifying date is 23 September 2007 so the £300 payment is made if the oldest person was born on 23 September 1927 or earlier and it is £200 if the oldest person was born on 23 September 1947 or earlier. It should be paid before Christmas, directly into your parent's bank or building society account, or by cheque sent to his home.

Your parent's household may get more than these amounts if there are more than two people aged 60 or more, or if two or more people are making separate claims for Pension Credit (a couple receiving Pension Credit counts as one joint claim).

The Winter Fuel Payment is not means-tested or taxable. Most people will automatically receive their Winter Fuel Payment and do not have to claim. But people aged 60–64 who do not get a retirement pension should claim the Winter Fuel Payment. Your parent does not have to be receiving any particular benefit to get a Winter Fuel Payment – qualification is simply by age.

Up to 40,000 people of this age do not get the payment each year.

If you think your parent should qualify for a Winter Fuel Payment but it has not arrived by the middle of December 2007, call the Winter Fuel Payments Helpline (see chapter 6).

GRANTS AND BENEFITS FOR PEOPLE WITH DISABILITIES

'It took 11 years for me to get my mobility allowance, though nothing in my condition had changed in that time.' (father)

'She was refused when we first applied, so I asked the social worker to go through the forms with us. Then she got it.' (daughter)

THE INDEPENDENT LIVING FUND

The Independent Living Fund helps severely disabled people pay for care services in their own home. To qualify, your parent must be under 65 or have been disabled since before the age of 65. In addition, your parent will have been assessed as needing a high level of care services from the local authority and also receive the highest rate of Disability Living Allowance care component. Contact your parent's local social services department if you think your parent may qualify.

DISABILITY BENEFITS

The main disability benefits are:

- Disability Living Allowance if your parent is under 65; and
- Attendance Allowance if your parent is 65 or over.

Attendance Allowance is a less generous entitlement than Disability Living Allowance, for which there is no justification. If you agree, you could write to your MP demanding that this situation is rectified. To claim Disability Living Allowance or Attendance Allowance, call the Benefits Enquiry Line or claim online (see chapter 6).

HOUSING GRANTS

Your parent may be able to get a grant or loan from the local council to help with the cost of home repairs or adaptations to make their home more suitable. The help available will depend on where your parent lives, on their finances and whether they are a home owner or a tenant. (See the section 'Care in your parent's home', page 55.)

You should also make sure that your parent is getting all the means-tested help that they are entitled to, such as Pension Credit, Housing Benefit and Council Tax Benefit. If your parent is receiving Pension Credit they may be able to claim a Community Care Grant. These grants can pay for items that your parent needs because of disability. But your parent cannot claim for an item that the local authority or the NHS should provide for him.

DISABILITY LIVING ALLOWANCE AND ATTENDANCE ALLOWANCE

Disability Living Allowance is a benefit paid to help with the extra costs of long-term illness or disability. To qualify for Disability Living Allowance, your parent must make a claim before their 65th birthday. Your parent's income and savings do not affect whether they can get Disability Living Allowance, or how much they get. Disability Living Allowance is split into two parts; claims can be made for either or both these components:

- care component for the help someone needs to look after themselves: it can be paid at one of three rates (lower, middle and higher);
- mobility component for the help someone needs to get around: it can be paid at one of two rates (lower or higher).

Attendance Allowance is a benefit paid to people aged 65 or over to help them with the extra costs of a long-term illness or disability as above. Again, income and savings do not affect whether your parent can get Attendance Allowance or how much they can get. Attendance Allowance is also paid at two rates (lower or higher), but the amount your parent will get depends on the amount of help needed. There is no amount for mobility needs in Attendance Allowance, but if your parent received the DLA mobility component when they turned 65, they can continue to claim it. Also, if their mobility difficulties began before their 65th birthday and they were getting the DLA care component at that time, they can claim for the mobility component later.

HELP WITH HEALTH CHARGES

'I am usually aware of the allowances that are available for people in my position, but the changes that are constantly made make it difficult to keep up to date.' (father)

'The doctor said I needed to see a chiropodist, but I'd have to wait so long, I probably wouldn't be able to walk by the time I got an appointment. So I just paid.' (mother)

- If your parent receives the guarantee credit part of Pension Credit, Income Support or income-based Job Seeker's Allowance they are automatically entitled to all 'health benefits': free prescriptions, dental treatment, sight tests and 'vouchers' for glasses or contact lenses, wigs and fabric supports as well as travel to hospital. They do not need to apply for this help. But if they receive only the savings credit part of Pension Credit they are not automatically entitled to these health benefits.
- If your parent gets a war disability pension, has a war pension exemption certificate and needs treatment because of the disability for which they get the pension, they are also automatically entitled to free prescriptions and wigs and fabric supports. They may also be able to get money back for dental treatment, sight tests and vouchers for glasses and hospital travel costs. For more information contact the Treatment Group (see chapter 6).
- If your parent is aged 60 or over, they are automatically entitled to free prescriptions and free sight tests. They may also be able to get help with other charges on grounds of low income. If they live in Wales or Scotland they will also be entitled to free dental examinations.
- If your parent does not automatically qualify for help with

other health costs but is over 60 and has a low income, they may still be able to get help with these charges unless they have substantial savings. They may get things such as dental care completely free, or they may pay a reduced charge. However, your parent does need to make a claim for this help.

■ Finally, even if your parent does not fall into any of the categories mentioned, they may be exempt from paying charges for particular treatments. For example, someone with diabetes would be entitled to a free sight test because of their diabetes, but would still have to pay all other charges, unless they were exempt for other reasons.

Where possible, it is best to apply for help with health charges before your parent actually needs the treatment. Otherwise, they may have to pay the full cost of the treatment and reclaim the money later, which is clearly less convenient (and in certain cases, refunds are not available). If your parent is not able to make the application for health reasons, you can do it on their behalf.

To apply for help with health charges, a form, HC1, needs to be completed. The form should be available from your local Jobcentre Plus office or by calling the Department of Health (see chapter 6). It is also stocked by hospitals and some doctors, dentists and opticians. The address to send it to is given on the form. If you have difficulty filling in the form for your parent, ask a Citizens Advice Bureau or call the Prescription Pricing Authority (PPA) Patient Services (see chapter 6), which can either help you to fill in the form over the phone or will complete the form on your parent's behalf and send it to them to check and sign.

The amount of money available will vary according to the applicant's financial situation, their age and state of health. If you have any queries about getting help with health costs or refunds if your parent has paid for a service and subsequently discovered that they should have had financial help, ring the PPA.

PRESCRIPTIONS

Everyone aged 60 and over automatically qualifies for free prescriptions. (In Wales everyone gets free prescriptions regardless of age.) Simply tick the relevant box on the back of the prescription and complete and sign the declaration before handing it over the counter at the chemist. Usually the prescription will have your parent's date of birth printed on it, but if it does not you will have to show proof that they are over 60. This can be done by showing an official document with your parent's name and date of birth on, such as an NHS medical card, driving licence or passport.

MEDICAL EXEMPTION CERTIFICATES

People with specified medical conditions can get free NHS prescriptions if they hold a valid medical exemption certificate. Forms to obtain a medical exemption certificate are available from doctors' surgeries. Of course, if your parent is over 60 they will already be eligible for free NHS prescriptions.

DENTAL TREATMENT

Dental treatment is not free for everyone and varies between England, Scotland, Wales and Northern Ireland. If your parent is not entitled to free NHS treatment, the amount they will be charged will depend on the treatment required. If your parent is concerned about how much their treatment will cost, they should ask the dentist how much it will be before it starts.

If a hospital dentist gives your parent dental treatment while they are staying in hospital they should not have to pay anything. If they are a patient of the Community Dental Service they will have to pay for dental treatment unless they are entitled to free treatment. They may also have to pay a charge for dentures and bridges.

Making a claim for dental treatment

In order to claim, your parent should tell the dentist's receptionist before treatment that they qualify for free or reduced-cost treatment.

Then they will simply have to tick a box on a form provided by the dentist. They will need to ensure that the dentist treats patients under the NHS as private dental treatment is not covered by the health benefits system. Remind your parent to take documents with them to show that they are entitled to free or reduced-cost treatment: for example, a benefit book, benefit award letter or Health Certificate form that they claimed through the HC1.

SIGHT TESTS AND GLASSES

NHS sight tests are free for everyone aged 60 and over.

Sight tests are vitally important because as well as being necessary for spectacle prescriptions they can detect a number of diseases at an early stage when they can be effectively treated. For this reason, it is recommended that your parent has a sight test from an ophthalmic optician (optometrist) or ophthalmic medical practitioner at least every two years – and more often if they notice any changes in their vision. Your parent is entitled to a free eye test once every 24 months if they are aged 60–70 or once every 12 months if they are over 70, unless the optician recommends that they have tests more often.

Note that if you are over 40 and either of your parents has been diagnosed with glaucoma, you and any other child of theirs is also eligible for a free sight test.

Making a claim for optical treatment

In order to claim, your parent should tell the optician before the sight test that they qualify for free or reduced-cost treatment. They will probably be asked for proof of their age to get the free sight test, so they should take along a birth certificate, driver's licence or passport to show the optician that they are over 60.

'Vouchers' for glasses or contact lenses

Even if your parent qualifies automatically for full help with health costs, the whole cost of glasses or contact lenses will probably not be covered. If your parent needs new glasses or contact lenses, they

FREE SIGHT TESTS

You parent is entitled to a free sight test if one of the following applies:

■ your parent is aged 60 or over; or

■ your parent's income is low enough; in which case they will need to complete form HC1 and send it to the Health Benefits Division of the Prescription Pricing Authority; or

■ your parent is registered blind or partially sighted; or

■ your parent has been prescribed complex or powerful lenses; or

■ your parent is diagnosed with diabetes or glaucoma; or

■ your parent is the brother, sister or child of a person with glaucoma; or

■ your parent is a Hospital Eye Service patient and has been sent to have a sight test by a medical consultant or doctor.

should fill in the GOS3 Optical Voucher form from their optician. The optician will issue a 'voucher' which can be used to help pay for glasses or contact lenses from any optician. The value of this voucher depends on the kind of glasses or contact lenses required.

The voucher may cover the cost of a suitable pair of lenses, but it will not cover all the frames available at an optician, and your parent may have to shop around. If they want more expensive frames, they will have to pay the difference between the value of the voucher and the cost of the frames.

Your parent is entitled to a voucher if he or she:

■ is automatically entitled to health benefits (see above) or

■ has been prescribed complex lenses.

If your parent is a Hospital Eye Service patient, and needs frequent changes of glasses or lenses, they only have to pay for the first pair.

They will also get a voucher to help with the cost of the first pair if they need complex lenses, or have an automatic entitlement.

Your parent may be able to get a voucher for the repair or replacement of lost or broken glasses if:

- your parent is ill and the PPA's Patient Services is satisfied that they would not have lost or damaged the glasses if they did not have that illness; and
- the cost is not covered by insurance or warranty; and
- your parent is entitled to a voucher because they receive the guarantee credit part of Pension Credit, Income Support, income-based Job Seeker's Allowance, Working Tax Credit or has been prescribed complex lenses.

Making a claim for replacement spectacles or contact lenses

Your parent simply needs to show the optician some proof that they are entitled to a voucher – for example, a Health Certificate, benefit award letter or a benefit book. The optician should then give your parent the voucher form GOS3 to fill in.

If your parent needs a voucher because they have lost or damaged their glasses ask for form GOS4.

WIGS AND FABRIC SUPPORTS

If your parent needs a wig or a fabric support (abdominal or spinal support or surgical brassiere) for medical reasons, help may be available for the cost of these items.

Your parent is entitled to free wigs and/or fabric supports if one of the following applies to you:

- your parent is automatically entitled to health benefits; or
- your parent is a hospital inpatient at the time the wig or fabric support is supplied.

Making a claim for a wig or fabric support

Your parent should tell the hospital when they go for a fitting if they are entitled to a free wig or fabric support, or help with part of the cost. Remind them to take proof of their entitlement.

TRAVEL TO HOSPITAL

Your parent may be able to claim a refund for the cost of travelling to and from hospital or other treatment centres that they are attending for NHS treatment under the Hospital Travel Costs Scheme (HTCS). The fares of an escort may also be paid if the hospital agrees that your parent needs someone to accompany them for medical reasons. Your parent will be expected to use the cheapest form of transport available.

MORE INFORMATION ON HEALTH BENEFITS

Two leaflets have details about health benefits:

- HC11, *Help with health costs*
- HC12, *Charges and optical voucher values.*

These are available from local benefit offices or can be requested by phoning the Department of Health, or contact the Prescription Pricing Authority (PPA) Patient Services (see chapter 6).

LASTING POWERS OF ATTORNEY

'You don't seem to come across much about powers of attorney. It was only after the death of my father that someone asked what would happen if my mother had a stroke too, but it wasn't fatal.' *(son)*

Your parents should be strongly advised to arrange for a lasting power of attorney in case they should for any reason become incapable of looking after their own affairs.

Until recently, your parent could arrange an enduring power of attorney (EPA), which allowed them to choose someone they trust, perhaps one of their children, to manage their financial affairs should they at some time in the future become unable to do so themselves, through dementia, illness or accident. As from 1 October 2007, the

EPA was replaced by lasting power of attorney (LPA) which, in addition to the financial matters mentioned above, also allows the chosen representative to make decisions concerning health and personal welfare. If, for example, your parent was unable to make a decision concerning medical treatment, the person who had agreed to be their LPA would make this decision for them.

Any EPA that was made before 1 October 2007 remains valid, but does not include decisions on medical treatment. This could prove difficult if, for example, there are children or other members of the family who cannot agree on a course of treatment. Perhaps you already hold an EPA for your mother. If she were to suffer a serious stroke you might be asked whether or not you wish her to be resuscitated if her condition were to deteriorate. Suppose you think her quality of life is too poor to warrant intrusive treatment but your brother thinks otherwise, wanting her life to be saved at all costs. Who makes the final decision?

However, if while your mother is still well you discuss what her wishes are for medical treatment should she fall seriously ill, you can replace the EPA with a LPA. You and your family will then have full knowledge, should the need ever arise, of her desires with regard to having active medical treatment or palliative care.

> Setting up an LPA could save you, your family
> and your parents a great deal of future heartache.

If either of your parents were to fall desperately ill tomorrow and become unable to communicate their needs without either an enduring or a lasting power of attorney being in place, their personal affairs would be placed in the care of the Court of Protection, also known as the Public Guardianship Office.

There are 55,000 clients registered with the Court of Protection who are deemed mentally incapable to act on their own behalf with regard to their finances. As they have not granted an EPA or LPA to anyone else, their affairs are placed under the jurisdiction of the Court.

The Court appoints a Receiver to act on the client's behalf in the everyday running of his or her affairs, and the Receiver is answerable to the Court.

In practice, if this were your father who had had a serious stroke and he held all your parents' money in his name, even your mother would have to ask the Receiver to release funds for her to carry out everyday financial matters. Not only would she and you have to come to terms with the grief and emotion of his illness, you would have the added strain of dealing with officials with regard to your father's affairs. Although you or your mother could apply to the Court to become the Receiver, this takes time and money. Even when you are appointed as a Receiver, you are still restricted by the Court as to how much money you can spend.

The Court of Protection plays a valuable role in safeguarding the interests of people who do not have close family or friends, but if at all possible you should ensure that your parent appoints someone they trust to deal with their affairs should they become unable to do so. Although the powers of an LPA or EPA become applicable only after a person is incapacitated, if your parent is at all concerned about signing away his or her rights, consult a solicitor. It is quite understandable that your parent may be frightened by the implication of a lasting power of attorney and effectively handing power over their money, property and even their life to someone else.

If you are appointed your parent's LPA, make sure that you know what their wishes are with regard to finances, property and future medical care. You may find this a difficult subject to bring up and will not want to offend or upset your parent, but to ensure that their wishes are fulfilled you need to know in detail what they want and this cannot be undertaken during a casual conversation over the phone or lunch. Explain to your parent that you only want what they want for their future and that you should both find the time to talk for long enough so that you are clear about their wishes. During the conversation, make notes so that you can refer back to any specific request at a future date, and keep these notes in a safe but accessible place.

LPA forms can be downloaded free of charge from the website: www.guardianship.gov.uk/formsdocuments/forms.htm or bought from solicitors or even from high street stationery chains.

LIVING WILLS OR 'ADVANCE STATEMENTS'

'I've got a living will because if I can't carry on looking after myself, I won't be very happy. I wouldn't want to carry on if I didn't know what was going on.' (*mother*)

A lasting power of attorney specifies who will look after your parent's assets and medical treatment if they are no longer able to do so. Another legally binding option with regard to medical treatment only is a living will (also known as an advance directive or statement).

Usually, a living will gives specific directions with regard to medical treatment should you fall ill. It can request life-sustaining treatment or refusal of treatment. It is legally binding provided that, at the time of signature, the person making it:

- has the mental capacity to make the medical decisions contained in the living will;
- understands the consequences of these decisions;
- makes clear their wishes as to future treatment (and the document covers the medical circumstances which later arise);
- makes the decision(s) voluntarily and not under somebody else's influence;

The living will may include your parent's wish to refuse antibiotics, tube feeding or resuscitation. On the other hand, it may say that your parent wishes to have life-sustaining treatment even if they have very little chance of recovery. Unlike a refusal of treatment, this type of request is not binding on the doctor, but at least he or she will know that your parent wants the chance to recover from their illness even if it is not very likely that they will do so.

While an LPA hands over blanket authority to someone else, the living will can be as detailed as your parent wishes with regard to medical treatment. It effectively allows your parent advance control in the case of incapacitating illness. It is based on the principle that all of us can refuse medical treatment if we do not want it and can offer elderly parents the peace of mind that if, in their opinion, their health deteriorates significantly and they are left with little quality of life, they will not be kept alive for longer than necessary.

Living wills can also set out a Health Care Proxy – someone that your parent would like the medical staff to consult on important decisions. Obviously, if you agree to be your parent's Health Care Proxy, it is crucial that you discuss in detail your parent's wishes with regard to medical treatment.

Living wills are recognised by all the professional nursing and medical organisations including the British Medical Association and the Royal College of Nursing. In theory, anyone can write a living will and sign it in the presence of witnesses (preferably including their doctor), to render it legal. However, it is advisable to consult a solicitor to ensure that it is properly drawn up and avoid any future problems.

MAKING A WILL

'After the death of my mother, I discovered that my father had all five of his children as executors for his will – a nightmare situation. He's drawn up a new one.' (*daughter*)

'What do I need a will for? I've not got much and what there is will go to my children.' (*mother*)

If your parent does not already have a will, you should encourage them to make one. Having one will ensure that your parent's estate is distributed as they would wish after their death.

Writing a will using an off-the-shelf form from a stationer's can be risky, and almost certainly will not be tax-efficient, so it is always best to seek specialist advice. The possibilities include expert wills and legacies advisers who work for charities and solicitors who specialise in wills and probate. The Law Society (see chapter 6) can provide a list of solicitors in the area where your parent lives.

Before instructing anyone to write a will, your parent should ask for a copy of their public liability insurance certificate and, if it is a solic-itor, their fees sheet, so that the cost can be clear from the outset.

Whatever the cost, it is bound to be less than if they do not make a will and the family subsequently have to engage professional help to sort out the estate after the individual's death.

Your parent can make a provision in their will for specific gifts to friends and family members as well as make clear their wishes with regard to any pets they may have, and express their preferences for what happens to their body (burial or cremation) and what sort of funeral, if any, they would like. In addition, they can leave legacies or bequests to charities that they support.

For a basic guide to making a will, see the Help the Aged website, order its free advice leaflet *Making a Will*, or contact its Wills Advice Service, which offers for free, confidential advice to anyone of state retirement age who wishes to make a will (see chapter 6 for details).

A key element of the will is the naming of one or more people to act as executors of the estate. These are people that your parent trusts to carry out their wishes as detailed in the will, who ideally have some knowledge and experience of financial matters, and who can reasonably be expected to outlive your parent. Executors should be given the authority to consult and pay professionals out of the estate for financial and legal advice.

Your parent will need to sign the will in the presence of witnesses to make it legally binding.

After writing a will, your parent can always make changes subse-quently if their circumstances change or if they simply have a change of heart. Any change or addition to a will is called a codicil and has to be witnessed in the same way as the original document.

The finalised will should be kept in a safe place and the executors should be made aware of where it is. Often people leave a copy with their solicitor, if they used one, or with their bank (though it can take a while to retrieve a will from a bank unless an executor has been introduced by the maker of the will beforehand). Another possibility is to store the will at the Principal Probate Registry, or at a will storage facility. Alternatively, it could be left with your parent's other important personal papers such as their birth certificate or passport. ■

4
HEALTH AND WELL-BEING

A BALANCED DIET

A healthy diet... provides energy and helps protect against illness during the winter months. There are also many... that... where a good balance of... help alleviate the symptoms... keep people often say that their health... diminish at this time of year...

'I think that as some people get older, they give up too easily and let others do things that they could easily manage themselves.' (*mother*)

'If I can't do something, I say so. When my granddaughter stays, I go to bed earlier.' (*mother*)

'I make sure that I eat properly but still notice that I'm not as strong as I was even a couple of years ago.' (*father*)

As our parents become older and frailer, it is tempting to do more and more for them even if they are still able to manage for themselves. We may believe that this is a kindness when, in fact, it is far better if our parents continue to do as much as possible for themselves. This not only helps them maintain their independence and dignity for longer, it also keeps their minds and bodies more active and healthy. If your parent has recently had a fall or been widowed, they may feel vulnerable and depressed, but instead of cosseting them you should encourage them with firm kindness to try hard to pick their lives up again.

As well as encouraging them to keep active and focused, there are many things you can do to try to maintain your parent's health.

A BALANCED DIET

A healthy diet gives provides energy, and helps protect against illness during the winter months. There are also many illnesses where a good balanced diet can help alleviate the symptoms. Older people often say that their appetite has diminished, but eating regular meals and snacks is a good habit. Encourage your parent to eat three meals a day, and in case they cannot get out to the shops for a few days due to bad weather or a bad back, make sure their store cupboards are kept well stocked. Meat, fish, fruit and vegetables, canned or frozen, cereals, wholegrain pasta and rice store well, as do long-life milk and various drinks.

Like everyone else, your parent should aim to eat at least five portions a day of fruit, vegetables and salads. They are full of vitamins, minerals and fibre which help the gut work effectively and so avoid constipation. They are also good as snacks throughout the day.

Twice a day, your parent should aim to include some meat, fish, eggs, nuts or beans. These foods contain proteins which help build and repair the body. Cakes and biscuits provide energy, but if your parent has a weight problem or any of a variety of illnesses, they should only be eaten sparingly. However, bread and cereals, especially wholegrain varieties, should be eaten with every meal.

Milk, cheese and yoghurt are rich in calcium and help keep bones strong. Your parent should eat three portions a day; low-fat dairy products still have all the goodness in them without the calories.

Finally, encourage your parent to drink plenty of liquid. Whether it is tea, coffee, fruit juice or milky drinks, they all aid digestion and help avoid constipation.

If your parent starts to lose a lot of weight, cannot keep food down or has severe constipation or diarrhoea, they should see their doctor promptly.

HOBBIES AND INTERESTS

One of the best things about retirement is that your parent should now have the time to take up new hobbies and pastimes. A good social life and meeting people with similar interests is enjoyable and keeps the mind active. For keen readers, the local public library will have details of book clubs and readings from published authors. If your parent likes books but has failing eyesight, remember that the library will also have a selection of audio (or 'talking') books and details of library services where recorded books can be delivered to their home. It will also have lists of local clubs, courses and meetings. Now may be a good time for your parent to come to grips with the internet, learn about their area's local history or even tackle the basics of a foreign language.

Many people meet their friends at work or through friends of their children, but as we get older these opportunities do not exist to the same degree. By joining a class or attending meetings, your parent will have the chance to make new friends. If they are not keen on the idea of going along alone, why not offer to go with them a couple of times to give them confidence in going somewhere new?

A HEALTHY MIND

Encourage your parent to do crosswords, word or number games, which are printed in many newspapers and magazines. Research published in 2003 found that solving crossword puzzles can significantly decrease the onset of dementia. Evidence showed that older people who did crosswords four days a week had a risk of dementia 47 per cent lower than among others who did puzzles once a week. It is suggested that other 'mind games' such as chess, draughts, backgammon, dominoes and mah-jong could have a similar effect.

KEEPING A PET

Animals provide companionship and need to be cared for. This can be very rewarding for an older person, making them feel less isolated as well as relieve stress and lower blood pressure. Nevertheless, keeping a pet is a responsibility, an expense and a commitment; it needs careful consideration. An alternative could be becoming a volunteer for the Cinnamon Trust (see chapter 6), an organisation that helps pet owners in several ways, including visiting dog owners who find it difficult to go out and take their dog out for walks.

VOLUNTEERING

There are many good reasons to encourage your parent to become a volunteer: making new friends, getting out of the house, putting something back into the community, learning new skills – to name but a few. Your parent's local church, temple, mosque or synagogue may have a volunteer programme that will appeal. In any case, there is a tremendous variety of volunteer projects in the UK and sure to be something to suit your parent. For more information, visit the RSVP (Retired and Senior Volunteer Programme) website (see chapter 6).

SOCIALISING WITH FRIENDS AND FAMILY

At first sight, it may seem odd to suggest that socialising with friends and family will help keep your parent healthier, but if they have something planned for most days, it will give their lives a purpose and a reason to get up each morning. Depression and frustration, linked to lethargy and low self-esteem, are major problems for many older people who live alone and can no longer live the full lives they once enjoyed. Any activity, family gathering or meal that they can look forward to, that keeps them cheerful and feeling loved and needed, is without doubt a benefit to their overall health.

KEEPING MOBILE AND ENGAGED WITH LIFE

'I've always walked and I'm sure it's good for me. I get offers, but as long as I can, I'd rather do my own garden.' (mother)

'We're obviously not as fast as we were before, but we still regularly play tennis.' (father)

'We gave up our car three years ago but we benefit from a frequent free bus service.' (father)

'I intend to always take the route requiring effort, and thereby lengthen my active life.' *(mother)*

REGULAR EXERCISE

Whatever age your parent is, regular, safe and enjoyable physical activity is essential for them to stay mobile and independent, and is the single most important thing they can do to maintain their health.

The many benefits include strengthening bones and maintaining heart and lung function. Also, exercise creates adrenalin, which makes people feel better and more positive. As a bonus, it can also be a way for your parent to meet different people and make new friends.

Your parent's local council or library will have details of a variety of clubs and activities available for older people in the area. Many local councils run classes especially for this age group, with some designed for those with medical conditions such as heart disease or arthritis; swimming pools often have specific times when they are open only for the over-60s.

BEING OVERWEIGHT

Being overweight makes it harder to enjoy exercise and may make other health problems, such as arthritis, worse. It can increase the risk of heart and chest troubles, diabetes, backache and varicose veins – all of which will affect mobility. If your parent needs to lose weight, get them to ask their doctor for help. Do not encourage them to skip meals or restrict their diet unless their doctor advises it. It is essential in later life to take in all the necessary nutrients for the body to work at its best.

WALKING

Encourage your parent to get out for a walk each day: a 20-minute walk will help maintain healthy heart and lungs. It can be part of their daily routine to do some shopping, visit the library, enjoy the park or drop in to see a friend. If, however, they have tired, aching feet or suffer from corns, ingrowing toenails or bunions, it will be more difficult.

Make sure that they have well-fitting shoes and that they talk to their doctor if they need to see a chiropodist.

Walking can be a gentle or exhilarating exercise that costs nothing. Do what you can to see that your parent makes the most of this simple activity.

HELP IN GETTING AROUND

If your parent suffers from a rheumatic disease, painful or stiff joints can seriously affect their mobility. Their doctor may be able to prescribe drugs or a physiotherapist may be able to offer help with special exercises. In addition, an occupational therapist may suggest a walking stick, frame or rollator (wheeled frame, usually with a basket attached). Walking sticks need to be of the correct length, so that the wrist creases when the arm is held by the side of the body. But if your parent needs two sticks for balance, they will need to be longer. Ask the occupational therapist for advice if you are concerned. All walking sticks need rubber ends, called 'ferrules', to make sure that they do not slip on the pavement or road. These wear out quickly and need to be checked regularly; they are easily replaced and can be bought from large chemists.

Walking frames give more support than a walking stick, are more stable and help to increase confidence. Rollators are easier to manoeuvre and do not break up the pattern of walking. They are good for people with moderate balance problems and can have detachable shopping bags fitted to them. All of these walking aids can be supplied free of charge by the NHS with referral from a doctor.

For information on wheelchairs and scooters or buggies, refer to the section on equipment for daily living (page 48).

PUBLIC TRANSPORT

In England, local councils offer free passes giving people aged 60 and over at least 50 per cent off bus fares and free local off-peak bus travel. In Northern Ireland, people aged 65 and over can get a pass offering free travel on buses and trains. In Scotland, people aged 60 and over are entitled to travel free on local buses at any time of day. In Wales, people aged 60 and over are entitled to free bus travel.

If your parent travels by train, they can apply for either a Senior Railcard or a Disabled Person's Railcard. With a railcard, most journeys are then purchased at a reduced rate. Application forms are available from main railway stations.

LOCAL TRANSPORT SCHEMES
Various local transport schemes rely on volunteer drivers, who often use their own cars to provide door-to-door services for older and disabled people. To find out about schemes in your parent's area, contact the Community Transport Association (see chapter 6).

DRIVING
If your parent has regularly driven throughout their adult life, it will be a blow to their independence and also their confidence when they decide that they are no longer safe on the roads. As a result, it is understandable that they may be reluctant to consider whether or not they still have adequate skills and sensory function. Nevertheless, if you are concerned about your parent's safety and the safety of other road users, you need to discuss the physical and mental changes that accompany ageing that can diminish the abilities of older drivers. The warning signs (see box) are not difficult to recognise.

BLUE BADGE PARKING SCHEME
If your parent is disabled and no longer able to walk any distance, their independence will be made much easier if they can still drive safely. To help them to get around, they are entitled to apply for a Blue Badge. Alternatively, if your parent is disabled and you, or someone else, drives for them, you may be entitled to apply for a Blue Badge on their behalf.

The Blue Badge (formerly known as the Orange Badge) allows people to park free at certain parking meters and in some pay-and-display bays. It also allows extended parking where there is usually a

TIME TO STOP DRIVING?

If any of the following apply to your parent's driving, you could bring up the possibility of considering alternative forms of transport:

- driving too fast or too slow
- not noticing pedestrians, cyclists or other vehicles
- ignoring, disobeying or misinterpreting street signs or traffic lights
- misjudging distances
- becoming easily frustrated and angry
- appearing drowsy, confused or frightened
- having frequent minor accidents or near-misses
- drifting across lane markings or bumping into kerbs
- performing dangerous manoeuvres, such as reversing the car into the middle of the road, without due care and attention
- forgetting to turn on headlights after dusk
- having difficulty turning the head, neck, shoulders or body while driving or parking.

When your parent does stop driving, make sure that they know about all the local transport options so that their social life outside the home remains as active as possible.

time restriction, and on single and double yellow lines, unless there is a ban on loading and unloading. You cannot park in bus or cycle lanes and must obey other parking regulations. The scheme does not apply on private land.

You should not be wheel-clamped if the badge (which may comprise two different items) is displayed correctly, though the police may remove your car if it is causing an obstruction. The disabled person can use the Blue Badge whether they are the driver of the vehicle or a passenger in their own or someone else's vehicle.

Some local authorities in tourist areas restrict their free parking in local car parks to residents only. It is always best to check the tariff boards in pay-and-display car parks to be sure.

Eligibility for the Blue Badge

You can qualify for a badge if you or the person you are caring for:

- gets the higher rate of the mobility component of the Disability Living Allowance (DLA), but this is only availabe for your parent if they became disabled before the age of 65;
- uses a car supplied by a government health department;
- receives a War Pensioners' Mobility Supplement.

Your parent may also qualify if they have a permanent and substantial disability which leaves them unable to walk, or if they have very considerable difficulty in walking.

A 'permanent and substantial disability' would mean that the person is generally incapable of visiting shops, public buildings and other places unless allowed to park close to the destination. Your parent (or you on their behalf) may be asked to answer a series of questions to enable your local authority to decide whether they are eligible. All the above will need to be verified by your parent's doctor.

Where to apply for the Blue Badge

Applications should be made to the social services or social work department of your local authority, which will decide whether your parent qualifies for a badge. If they do, they may also qualify for exemption from paying car tax (vehicle excise duty exemption). Unfortunately there is no right of appeal in the case of an unsuccessful application.

In London Blue Badge holders qualify for a 100 per cent exemption from the congestion charge, but must register with Transport for London (TfL) (see chapter 6), before travelling. An application form is available from TfL.

MOTABILITY AGREEMENTS

Motability is an organisation which helps people use the higher rate of the mobility component of the Disability Living Allowance to purchase or lease a suitable car, wheelchair or scooter.

Your parent's DLA mobility component may not cover all the costs. They may have to pay a deposit or for the cost of adaptations. And they will have to pay for some of the running costs. Check exactly what your parent will need to pay before they make a commitment.

For enquiries about the purchase or lease of a suitable car, call Motability; for enquiries about purchasing or leasing a wheelchair or scooter call route2mobility (see under Motability in chapter 6 for both numbers).

HOLIDAYS

Everyone needs a break and a chance to get away from their daily routine. Your parent may be nervous about going on holiday alone, but if you care for them on a regular basis it will be good for you to have some time alone, or with your partner (and/or children, if you have them). Perhaps you have siblings or other family members who would be willing to invite your parent for a holiday. They do not need to be going away – a stay at their home will be a break for you and your parent.

However, for an older person who wishes to be more adventurous, there are holiday companies specialising in trips for older and single travellers. (Help the Aged publishes an information sheet, *Holidays*, on this subject.) These trips may be organised round an activity such as painting or walking, or alternatively offer tours of historic or geographic interest. If your parent would like to meet a like-minded person to travel with, an organisation called Companions2Travel (see chapter 6) can, for a fee, put them in touch with someone with similar interests.

For people with disabilities, an organisation called Tourism for All offers holiday and travel information to them, their carers and people on low incomes. Again, see chapter 6.

TRAVELLING ABROAD

From the age of 77, your parent can get a free 10-year UK passport. For more information call the UK Passport Service adviceline (see chapter 6).

Your parent's entitlement to free medical treatment abroad will depend on which country they are visiting. Information about this is in a leaflet, *Health Advice for Travellers* (see under 'H' in chapter 6), available at the post office.

Within the European Economic Area (EEA) and Switzerland, British travellers are entitled to the same health care as the nationals of the country where they are staying. To obtain treatment, your parent will need a European Health Insurance Card (EHIC), which can be claimed using the leaflet mentioned above. However, this does not mean that your parent will be repatriated if they fall ill, nor will they automatically get free health care. Countries within the EEA have different health policies, and the EHIC merely offers treatment on the same basis as it would for an insured person living in that country. It is always advisable to make sure that medical insurance is obtained before travelling abroad; if your parent needs to see a doctor or have treatment while away, they must keep all receipts to make a claim.

COMMON ILLNESSES AND DISORDERS OF LATER LIFE

DEMENTIA

Dementia is a decline of mental function, including loss of memory. It affects all areas of the mind, making it difficult to concentrate or work out problems and can change a person's behaviour and personality. It can be extremely distressing to look after someone who has dementia, which tends to be a disorder of later life.

It affects five people in 100 over the age of 65, although for those over the age of 80 this increases to 20 per cent.

It is possible to suffer from dementia as a result of brain injury, as well as chronic alcoholism, but the most common form is Alzheimer's disease. It is estimated that currently approximately 400,000 people in Britain suffer from Alzheimer's disease, and by 2031, as people live longer, the number is expected to rise to 1.5 million.

Dementia symptoms

Every person with dementia is affected differently and the way they behave can depend on many factors such as their personality, physical condition and the type of dementia they have. Most people affected by dementia have some (but not all) of the symptoms described in the box. In the early stages of dementia, however, it can be quite hard to pinpoint exactly what the symptoms are. You may wonder about your parent if they start to suffer from a lack of concentration and seem unable to make decisions, or rather forgetful and confused. They may also get puzzled and upset about their behaviour.

There may be very obvious changes in your parent's behaviour or they may be very subtle and go unrecognised for some time. The first sign of dementia is usually loss of short-term memory. The person repeats what they just said or forgets where they put something just a few minutes ago. Other symptoms and signs are listed in the box.

If you are caring for a person with dementia who is close to you, your relationship will change greatly as time passes. You are likely to experience feelings of grief and bereavement as the illness progresses, not just in the period after the person's death. There are so many changes that occur along the way when caring for someone with dementia that it can be difficult for carers to deal with their feelings. You may adapt and come to terms with one stage of the person's illness only to find that their behaviour alters or their abilities decline further and your grieving starts all over again.

Most people with dementia will need a lot of support and specialist care, particularly in the final stages. Some services and activities are organised in the community particularly for people suffering from dementia, such as day care groups and lunch clubs. Following your parent's Care Assessment, their care manager should have information about what is available and appropriate for their needs.

POSSIBLE SIGNS OF DEMENTIA

- difficulty in finding words: sometimes people are able to compensate by using another word with the same meaning, or defining the word;
- forgetting names, appointments, or whether or not they have done something;
- more things than usual seem to go missing;
- difficulty in performing familiar tasks like driving or cooking a meal, household chores or managing personal finances;
- an abrupt personality change: for example, a previously sociable person might become withdrawn, or a quiet person might become coarse or silly;
- uncharacteristic behaviour: for example, your child's doting grandparent might become a continually grumpy one;
- mood swings, often with brief periods of anger and rage that have never previously been witnessed;
- clumsiness or poor judgement;
- behaviour disorders: paranoia and suspiciousness;
- a drop in general level of functioning and independence, though still coping with the daily routine at home;
- confusion and disorientation in unfamiliar surroundings: away from home, the person might wander off, trying to return to familiar surroundings.

Conditions such as a kidney infection, thyroid gland deficiency or a stroke can lead to someone displaying 'dementia-like' symptoms. A reaction to some types of medication can also cause these symptoms. So it is always important to see a doctor if someone starts showing signs of any of these symptoms as it may not be dementia they are suffering from but an illness that can be treated.

If your parent develops Alzheimer's disease or any other form of dementia, you will naturally be very distressed as the illness progresses.

If you have young children, they too will be disturbed, and while you are worrying about your parent it is easy to forget how anxious and confused your children may feel about their grandparent's behaviour. Do not assume that because they are young they will not notice. Children need clear explanations and reassurance in order to cope with the changing situation. It is also quite likely that as well as worrying about their grandparent, they will be concerned about you too.

Further information is available from the Alzheimer's Society (see chapter 6).

CANCER

Half of all cancers first appear in people aged over 70. If your parent mentions that they have noticed any change in their body, an unexplained upset stomach or change in bowel movements, encourage them to talk to their doctor.

In contrast to the rest of Europe, people in the UK tend to have a more advanced stage of breast and bowel cancer by the time they are treated. There may be several explanations for this but one may be the national characteristic, particularly among older people, of not wanting to bother the doctor.

Health problems can be frightening and cancer is possibly the biggest taboo of all, but the fact is that the earlier cancer is diagnosed, the better the chance of making a full recovery. Do not let your parent put changes down to their age or let them ignore the problem. No one is ever too old to be treated for any condition and that includes treatment for cancer.

Make sure your parent sees a doctor if they notice:

- a lump, or a sore which does not heal, including one in the mouth
- a mole which changes in shape, size or colour
- any abnormal bleeding
- a persistent cough or hoarseness
- changes in bowel movements
- any unexplained weight loss.

Speaking up and asking for clear information or a second opinion could be a very important first step to getting treatment.

Further information for people living with cancer can be found on the Cancerbackup website (see chapter 6); this charity also runs a free helpline staffed by specialist nurses who can provide information on all types of cancer and treatment, practical advice and emotional support.

DIABETES

Diabetes is a dangerous condition that can increase the chance of a stroke, heart disease, blindness and fatal kidney problems. If your parent is diagnosed with diabetes it means that the amount of glucose in their blood is too high.

This happens because the body cannot use the glucose properly. Glucose is a sugar; it is our prime source of energy and our brains cannot function without it. Our digestive system turns the carbohydrates that we eat into glucose. This is then distributed throughout the body by the bloodstream (hence the term 'blood sugar'). Spare glucose is stored in the liver and in muscles and it is also stored as fat.

Keeping the correct level of glucose in the blood is vital. This is the job of insulin, which is a hormone produced in the pancreas.

There are two main types of diabetes:

- type 1, in which the pancreas produces no insulin;
- type 2, in which the pancreas produces insufficient insulin, or it produces enough but it is not used properly by the body.

Type 1 diabetes is usually identified in childhood or early adulthood. It is treated through diet, exercise and daily insulin injections.

Type 2 diabetes, the most common form, usually affects older people, although it is becoming more common in the general population. It can be treated through diet and exercise and also through tablets and occasionally insulin injections.

The aim of treatment is to keep glucose levels and blood pressure at normal levels.

Signs and symptoms

The most common symptoms of diabetes are listed in the box (however, it is possible to develop the disease without having any of them):

DIABETES SYMPTOMS

- needing to pass water often, particularly at night
- being thirsty most of the time, or hungry
- unexpectedly losing weight
- lacking energy, feeling tired and drowsy
- having blurred vision
- tingling or numbness in legs, feet or fingers
- recurring skin, gum and/or urinary tract infections
- slow-healing cuts and bruises
- frequent itching of skin and/or genitals.

Most people have Type 2 diabetes for several years before being diagnosed. By the time they find out, at least a third are already showing signs of damage to the eyes, kidneys, nerves and heart, which result from too much sugar in the bloodstream.

Spotting diabetes early means that serious complications are much less likely to occur. If your parent displays any of the symptoms above, a simple blood test at the doctor's surgery will confirm whether or not they have diabetes.

Serious complications

Diabetes can lead to a range of serious complications. These include:

Eye disease 'Diabetic retinopathy' can cause blindness and is caused by damage to the small blood vessels at the back of the eye.

Coronary heart disease Having diabetes makes developing coronary heart disease more likely. Raised glucose levels can contribute to the narrowing and hardening of arteries.

Stroke Having persistently high glucose levels can also affect the arteries that supply the brain and make having a stroke more likely.

Foot problems Nerve damage and poor circulation mean that 15 per cent of people with diabetes develop foot ulcers. Ulcers can take time to heal. If they become infected and gangrenous this may lead to amputation.

Kidney disease 'Diabetic nephropathy' is one of the most serious complications of diabetes. High levels of glucose in the blood damages the small blood vessels in the kidneys, which can lead to kidney failure and death. Many people with diabetes need dialysis and kidney transplantation.

The following are risk factors for diabetes:

- being overweight makes developing Type 2 diabetes much more likely, and so does inactivity. In fact, the more overweight and unfit you are, the greater your risk of diabetes.
- diabetes tends to run in families, so if a close relative has diabetes your parent is more likely to develop it – as are you.
- age is also a factor: Type 2 diabetes is more common among older people.
- if your family originates from an African-Caribbean or South Asian background you are 3–5 times more likely to have diabetes than people with a European background.
- finally, women who have given birth to large babies or who developed temporary 'gestational' diabetes when they were pregnant are more likely to develop Type 2 diabetes.

Taking control of the situation

Diabetes can lead to serious complications, but a positive approach to controlling it can help to keep you healthy. As part of a positive approach, diabetics should:

Eat a healthy diet There is no such thing as a 'special' diet for people with diabetes. The best general advice is to eat less salt, sugar and fat, have at least five portions of fruit and vegetables a day, and base meals on starchy foods, such as bread, potatoes, pasta and rice.

Most people with Type 2 diabetes are overweight, but losing weight makes it easier to control diabetes. As the weight comes off, the resistance to insulin will improve, making it easier to control blood glucose levels. If your parent is diagnosed with diabetes they should be referred to a registered dietician, who will help explain what changes need to be made to eating habits.

Become more active Regular physical activity is good for your parent's overall health and can play a key role in helping to control diabetes. Exercise needs to be done regularly in blocks of at least half an hour and people with diabetes should aim to exercise at least every three days because the effects of exercise wear off. (See 'Keeping mobile', page 134, for more information.) But your parent should check with their GP or diabetes nurse before taking up exercise, particularly if they are overweight.

Stop smoking Smoking is particularly dangerous for people with diabetes. If they continue to smoke they are much more likely to have a heart attack or stroke. Among other things, smoking:

- raises blood sugar levels
- hampers the body's ability to use insulin
- doubles the likelihood of having problems with healing.

Follow a treatment plan Your parent will probably see a range of different healthcare workers, including their GP, a consultant diabetologist, dietician and diabetes specialist nurse. These people and others make up your parent's diabetes 'care team'. They should work with your parent to develop a programme of care that suits.

For more detailed information about diabetes management and treatment, visit the Diabetes UK website (see chapter 6). The organisation also has information about what diabetes care is available and what kind and level of care you should expect from the NHS.

HEARING

Most people who experience hearing loss as they get older do so due to a condition called presbyacusis, caused by wear and tear to the tiny hair cells in the inner ear. More than 50 per cent of people over 60 are affected by some type of hearing loss.

Your parent, aware that their hearing is deteriorating, may tell you, or you may notice one or more of the following common symptoms:

- your parent has difficulty understanding you if there is any background noise;
- if you phone your parent, they ask you to speak louder;
- your parent has the radio or TV on at high volume.

Other ear problems include:

Dry skin and earwax As a person gets older, their skin produces less moisture. This leads to dryer earwax, which can get stuck and cause a physical obstruction that can affect hearing. Dry earwax can also cause itchiness.

A build-up of earwax should be removed by a doctor or practice nurse to ensure that it is not pushed into the eardrum, where it can cause an inflammation or infection.

Dry or scratched skin in the outer ear can become inflamed. This can be painful and can lead to a watery discharge but eardrops from the doctor should alleviate the problem.

Ménière's disease If your parent complains of deafness, buzzing and a loss of balance, these may be symptoms of Ménière's disease, a problem with the inner ear that becomes more common with age. It is linked to a build-up of fluid in the inner ear, but the exact cause is unknown. Symptoms may fluctuate over time and the condition itself can come and go, with weeks or years between each bout.

Treatments can include drugs and a low-salt diet or an operation for more severe cases.

Ostosclerosis This is a condition in which the tiny bones of the middle ear, which normally move to transmit sound, become less mobile. It causes gradual hearing loss. This condition can run in families, it tends to start at around 30 years of age and affects more women than men.

Hearing aids can help to treat the hearing loss. An operation can help to restore hearing when the condition becomes severe.

Tinnitus Some people hear noises such as buzzing, ringing, hissing and roaring in their ears or head. This is called tinnitus. Among many different causes are injuries to the ear, hearing loss, stress, the impact of loud noise and some diseases of the ear. Sometimes tinnitus can occur for no apparent reason.

Strategies for managing tinnitus include relaxation techniques and avoiding absolute quiet. The Royal National Institute for the Deaf (RNID) runs a tinnitus helpline (see chapter 6).

Vertigo The inner ear is involved in controlling our balance and vertigo can be caused by degeneration of the inner ear's semicircular canals. With vertigo, people may feel that either they or their surroundings are constantly moving. It is most often a spinning sensation, but there may be a feeling that the ground is tilting.

Many medical conditions can cause dizziness; if your parent's GP is unable to make a specific diagnosis, a referral to a specialist may be necessary.

If your parent experiences hearing loss the first step is an appointment with your parent's GP, who should offer a referral to the ear, nose and throat (ENT) department of the local hospital for treatment.

Let other family members and friends know about your parent's hearing difficulty in order that they can make allowances. If the hearing loss is serious, the local social services or social work department should have a social worker for deaf people – contact the department for help and support.

Let your parent know that they should not feel guilty about their loss of hearing – it is not their fault. Encourage them to let other people know that they have a hearing problem and to ask them to speak clearly and slowly. Your parent should make sure that they can see people's faces clearly and watch facial expressions to help them understand what is being said; they should not feel embarrassed to ask people to repeat what they have said.

For further information on hearing problems visit the RNID website (see chapter 6).

COMMUNICATING WITH YOUR HEARING-IMPAIRED PARENT

- Start talking only when you are sure you have your parent's attention.
- If possible, reduce any background noise or other distractions.
- Face the light so your face is not in shadow.
- Speak clearly and naturally without raising your voice or over-emphasising words, and use natural lip movements and facial expressions
- Keep your hands away from your face and stay visible while talking.
- Repeat or, better still, rephrase things if your parent is finding it hard to understand what you are saying.
- Be patient and take your time to communicate properly.

HEART DISEASE, HIGH BLOOD PRESSURE AND HIGH CHOLESTEROL

The coronary arteries supply the tissues of the heart with blood, which carries oxygen. Coronary heart disease develops when the heart muscle stops working well because there are problems with its supply of blood and oxygen. It is the most common cause of premature death in the UK among people over 50.

The main cause of coronary heart disease is blockages in the arteries due to a sludgy build-up of sticky cholesterol, old muscle cells and clumps of blood platelets. This is called atherosclerosis, a condition which makes it difficult for the blood to flow and for its nutrients to be absorbed.

Symptoms and treatments for heart problems

Angina usually feels like a tightness or heaviness in the chest, but the feeling might spread further – say, to the arms, neck or stomach. The pain usually goes away within 10–15 minutes.

Angina is caused by insufficient oxygen reaching the heart muscle, because of the blockages in the coronary arteries. Physical exertion is likely to bring on an angina attack, as the heart must work harder and will therefore need more oxygen. There is a wide range of treatments for angina, including a small daily dose of aspirin to reduce the risk of a heart attack.

Glyceryl trinitrate (GTN) is prescribed to ease the pain of an angina attack. It is available in many forms, including tablets, sprays, patches and injections. These treatments will not clear the blockages once they have formed.

Surgical procedures developed to clear blocked arteries include angioplasty and coronary artery bypass graft. Further information on tests and treatments for coronary heart disease is on the British Heart Foundation website (see chapter 6).

Heart attack or myocardial infarction occurs when the blood supply to a part of the heart muscle is interrupted or stops, usually because of a blood clot in the coronary artery. Without oxygen the heart begins to shut down. The symptoms are usually, but not always, a crushing pain in the chest, which may spread to both arms (particularly the left) and up into the throat and jaw. If this does not go away within 15 minutes, help should be sought immediately by phoning 999 for an ambulance.

Cardiac arrest is the cessation of the heart's pumping action, a potentially fatal condition. Damage to the heart muscle (caused by a heart attack) can lead to the lower chambers quivering rather than beating in time with the rest of the heart. This is called ventricular fibrillation, which leads to cardiac arrest, when blood stops being delivered to the rest of the body. If cardiac arrest occurs, the heart will survive only if given a jolt of electricity (defibrillation).

Valvular heart disease The valves that separate the different chambers of the heart can become stiff and difficult to open or liable to leak. This reduces the efficiency of the heart as a pump and is known as valvular heart disease. When valves do not open properly the condition is called stenosis; when they leak it is called valve incompetence or regurgitation. Both can lead to heart failure.

Most cases of valvular heart disease can be detected with a stethoscope because the abnormal blood flow often produces a sound called a heart 'murmur'. Not all murmurs are abnormal or the result of heart disease.

Causes of heart conditions

- **Congenital heart disease** Some people have malformed heart valves when they are born but start to notice problems only as they get older (because their heart has to work harder). Abnormal valves are more likely to become infected: this is known as endocarditis. Infections can also make leaks more likely.
- **Rheumatic fever** Most sore throats are caused by viruses, but some are caused by a bacteria called streptococcus, which in turn can cause rheumatic fever. This is an inflammation of connective tissues throughout the body such as those in our joints, skin and also our hearts. Rheumatic fever can damage the delicate structure of heart valves. Due to the discovery and use of antibiotics, rheumatic fever is now far less common in the UK than it was in the past. However, older people and people who grew up in developing countries may have been affected by it. If you know that your parent has had rheumatic fever they will need regular examinations to ensure that their heart valves are undamaged.
- **Weakening of the heart** Heart attacks, infections and disease of the muscle itself can weaken the heart muscle. As we get older, our heart valves can become less supple and therefore more likely to leak.

Treatment Medications are often quite effective in treating cases of valvular regurgitation; however, stenotic valves generally require surgical procedures. Control of high blood pressure can be particularly important for people with valvular heart disease. Additionally drugs that thin the blood may be prescribed to reduce the likelihood of clots forming.

Arrhythmias and atrial fibrillation Irregular heartbeats or arrhythmias cause the heart to pump less effectively. Atrial fibrillation is a particular kind of irregular heartbeat that becomes more common with age; it affects 3–5 per cent of people over 70 and can increase the risk of stroke.

There may not be any symptoms, but your parent may be aware of an irregular or rapid heartbeat for several minutes or possibly hours. These palpitations can become permanent.

Treatments vary, but can include aspirin or anti-coagulation medication such as warfarin. An electrical current can be used to help the heart return to a normal rhythm and surgery might be appropriate for severe cases.

Heart failure is a general term used when the heart muscle is weak and unable to pump blood efficiently. The heart is still working, but it is not doing its job of supplying oxygen to the rest of the body properly. Symptoms include feeling tired all the time, becoming breathless very easily, and swollen ankles.

Heart failure affects about one in ten of people aged over 65. It usually results from a heart attack or years of high blood pressure and coronary heart disease.

Current treatments for heart failure can relieve symptoms and slow the progression of the condition. Medication may include diuretics, beta blockers and ACE (angiotensin converting enzyme) inhibitors.

Smoking and heart problems

People who smoke have twice the risk of a heart attack of those who do not.

The carbon monoxide smokers take in reduces the ability of the blood to carry oxygen to the heart and all other parts of the body. Nicotine stimulates the body to produce adrenaline, which makes the heart beat faster and raises the blood pressure, causing the heart to work harder.

Smoking also increases the clumping of blood platelets that makes blockages in the arteries (atherosclerosis) more likely as well as increasing the chances of blood clots. All in all, your parent is making life very difficult for their heart if they smoke. The good news is that the benefit to the heart starts as soon as they stop smoking.

Cholesterol levels

Cholesterol is one of the body's fats. We need it to build cells, make hormones and produce energy. But when there is too much in your blood, it contributes to the hardening and narrowing of the arteries (atherosclerosis), which is one of the main causes of coronary heart disease.

What most people do not realise is that very little cholesterol comes from food. What really matters is the amount of saturated fat that you eat, because your body then turns this into cholesterol.

There are two sorts of cholesterol: a 'bad' sort called low-density lipoprotein (LDL) and a 'good' sort called high-density lipoprotein (HDL), which actually protects against atherosclerosis. It is the proportion of bad cholesterol to good cholesterol that is important for keeping your heart healthy.

The level of 'bad' cholesterol can be lowered by eating a low-fat diet and, if necessary, taking medication. Exercising can raise 'good' cholesterol.

People with normal levels of cholesterol, suffering from either heart disease or stroke, may be given cholesterol-lowering drugs as part of their treatment.

High blood pressure

To get round the body, blood has to be under considerable pressure. If the pressure of blood in the arteries is too high there is a greater risk of hardened and blocked arteries (atherosclerosis) and a greater chance of stroke, kidney disease and general heart problems.

High blood pressure is also known as hypertension. Anyone with a blood pressure measurement that is consistently more than 140/90mmHg has high blood pressure.

However, most people could do with lowering their blood pressure. This can be done through having a healthier diet, more exercise, less salt and drinking sensibly. For more information see the beginning of this chapter.

People from south Asian or African-Caribbean backgrounds

People of south Asian extraction – from India, Bangladesh, Pakistan and to a lesser degree Sri Lanka – have some of the world's highest rates of death from coronary heart disease. A genetic predisposition is to blame for this high rate of heart problems.

African-Caribbean people are more likely to have diabetes and high blood pressure, leading to further health conditions such as stroke and heart problems, than people from a European background. It is not exactly clear why this is; it may be a combination of social and biological factors.

Although ethnic origin cannot be changed, do not think that nothing can be done about this risk factor. If you are from a south Asian or African-Caribbean background it makes sense for you and your parent to reduce your chance of developing heart disease by reducing your other risk factors.

Is heart disease different for women?

Until the menopause women have less risk of heart disease than men, but the hormonal changes that happen at that time take away the natural protection, leaving women vulnerable to the affects of atherosclerosis and other causes of heart problems.

Research shows that women underestimate the likelihood of developing heart disease and may therefore ignore advice about how to prevent it. A British Heart Foundation survey found that most women thought that breast cancer was a bigger threat to their health. But statistics show that women are four times more likely to die from heart disease than breast cancer.

Visit the British Heart Foundation's website (see chapter 6) for more information.

INCONTINENCE

Dealing with wet or messy nappies or pants is an aspect of parenting that we accept with young children. However, as people grow up, loss of bladder or bowel control is associated with a lack of hygiene and control. Coping with a parent's incontinence is stressful for both parties. From a young age, we are trained to control our bodily urges and to use a toilet when we need to: losing this control is frightening for your parent. It can affect self-esteem and dignity. Nobody wants to be incapable of looking after their own toileting needs and neither do we, as adult children, particularly want to be responsible for wiping our parent's bottom. It can be humiliating for all concerned and there is no easy answer on coping mechanisms.

Getting rid of our body's waste products is a complex process. When our control mechanisms do not work properly we experience incontinence: the accidental or involuntary leakage of urine or bowel movements. This can have an impact on confidence and well-being as well as on personal hygiene and health.

Although incontinence is an awkward problem, it is also extremely common. Approaching the issue with good humour and matter-of-factness can improve the embarrassment for you and your parent. As it is a common problem, a lot of help is available and there may be some medical treatment available for your parent.

There are two types of incontinence:

- urinary: loss of control of the bladder; and
- faecal: loss of control of the bowel.

Although bowel and bladder weakness becomes more common as we get older, incontinence is not an inevitable part of ageing. But if your parent suffers from incontinence, it may become something that happens occasionally, frequently or all the time.

Urinary incontinence is far more common than faecal incontinence. It can be:

- **stress incontinence**, which happens when someone coughs, sneezes or takes exercise; this is caused by a weakness in the muscles that control the opening of the bladder and pelvic floor; or
- **urge incontinence**, which occurs when someone has a sudden urge to pass urine but is unable to reach the toilet in time; or
- **overflow incontinence**, which happens when the bladder does not empty completely; or
- **functional incontinence,** whereby someone has difficulty getting to the toilet or undoing clothing quickly enough.

Whatever the cause, you need to get your parent an appointment with the doctor.

If the incontinence does not respond to treatment, there are practical ways of helping people feel more comfortable and protecting their clothes and bedding. Ask your parent's GP for a referral to a continence adviser.

- It is a good idea to put a waterproof protector under your parent's bottom sheet as well as a soft absorbent pad under their body. Disposable ones can be obtained through your parent's district nurse; washable pads can be bought from specialist suppliers. They enable your parent to sit or lie on a dry surface.
- Special protective duvet covers and pillowcases are also available.
- Incontinence pants and pads can be worn day and night. You need to make sure that they are adequately absorbent and are changed as often as necessary to avoid the skin from chafing. If your parent spends a lot of time sitting, you need to be particularly careful about the sacral area at the bottom of their back; this is a very common place for pressure sores to develop.

CONDITIONS THAT MAY CAUSE URINARY INCONTINENCE

- Urinary tract infections that usually respond to treatment with medication
- Prostate gland problems, which affect men and may be treated by an operation
- Side-effects of medication, which can be alleviated by a change of prescription
- Severe constipation, which can put pressure on the bladder and also lead to some loose faecal incontinence. Anyone with this problem should be encouraged to follow a diet that contains plenty of fibre, take regular exercise and drink plenty of liquids to help prevent the constipation.

- If incontinence is a problem during the daytime, too, it may be advisable to replace carpet with vinyl flooring and ensure that your parent's clothes are easily removable in case of an urgent need for the loo or accident.

Incontinence is not an inevitable symptom of dementia but is quite common as someone with dementia may simply forget to go to the toilet, forget where the toilet is or mistake something else, such as an armchair, for the toilet. Leaving the loo door open so that your parent can see it may help, as will a routine of reminding them to go to the loo.

Whatever the reason for your parent's incontinence and however frustrating you find it, do try:

- not to be angry;
- to overcome any distaste or embarrassment you feel;
- to remember that it is not your parent's fault: they are not doing it on purpose or to upset you.

It is also important to ensure good personal hygiene as incontinence can lead to skin irritation that may make your parent feel generally uncomfortable. If they have an accident, help them to wash with mild soap and warm water and dry them carefully before putting on fresh pads and clothes. Wash soiled clothes or bedding immediately or soak them in an airtight container until they are washed, to save unpleasant odours. As with a child's nappy, dispose of your parent's used pad appropriately.

If you are struggling to deal with your parent's continence problems, discuss them with the district nurse or continence adviser. The Continence Foundation is a charity that works to provide information and offer expertise on all aspects of incontinence.

Another charity, InContact, is for people affected by bladder and bowel problems. It provides support and information, and represents the interests of people with continence problems. Both organisations have helpful websites.

INFLUENZA

Immune systems decline with age, which is why the risk of flu (influenza) is a serious issue for older people.

Flu is a virus that affects the cells in the lungs. There are many types of flu virus, and they change frequently. Flu can be caught at any time of the year, but the most common time is between December and March. It spreads through droplets released into the air when someone who has it coughs or sneezes.

Flu is more than just a cold. In older people it also makes the possibility of pneumonia and other potentially serious and fatal complications more likely.

The Department of Health specifically recommends vaccination for people who are in a 'high-risk' group.

High-risk groups
The groups who are considered to be at a high risk from flu include:
■ people aged 65 and over;

- people with respiratory disease such as bronchitis, asthma and emphysema;
- people with heart disease, kidney disease or diabetes;
- people whose immune system is weak because of disease or treatment; and
- residents of care homes or other long-stay care accommodation.

Symptoms of flu

The typical symptoms of flu are a high temperature (103°F or 39.4°C) with chills, a cough, sore throat, general weakness, painful muscles, backache and headache.

The major difference between flu and the common cold is that an older person may be 'knocked flat' by flu, unable to do anything but go to bed until the worst of the illness has passed.

The main symptoms of flu generally last for about seven days. For some people, however, complications such as bronchitis and pneumonia will delay recovery. Once the severe illness has passed, your parent may find that they still feel tired and unwell. This could last for several weeks.

Flu vaccination

Vaccines are available every year from October and your parent should have one. Flu should be avoided if at all possible and the vaccine prevents the illness for about three-quarters of people who are vaccinated. If your parent does catch flu, they will have a milder illness with fewer complications than if they had not been vaccinated.

The flu jab should be easily available from your parent's GP surgery.

Recovering from flu

After a bout of flu, many people feel tired or under the weather for several weeks. Encourage your parent to get plenty of rest but also to take a daily walk. Nourishing food is important; if your parent has

CARE OF AN OLDER PERSON WITH FLU

Flu is debilitating and an older person who has it will need a lot of looking after. Antibiotics are of no use although they may be used to treat infections, which can develop as a result of flu. Symptoms may be treated as follows.

- Encourage your parent to stay in bed and rest. Give plenty to drink of non-alcoholic fluids to replace the liquid lost through sweating.
- Aspirin, paracetamol or anti-inflammatory drugs such as ibuprofen can relieve headaches, muscle pains and fever.
- Cough medicines and decongestants can be helpful. But if your parent is already taking other medications, whether prescribed or bought over the counter, always ask a pharmacist's advice.
- If your parent feels very hot and feverish, sponging down with tepid water can reduce body temperature.
- Encourage your parent to eat what they can.

Let your parent's GP know about their condition and if symptoms do not subside in a week or you are worried about wheezing or breathlessness, make sure the doctor knows.

If your parent lives alone and you are visiting daily, let their neighbours know that they are unwell so that they too can check on your parent when you are not around.

a poor appetite, meal replacement drinks can provide a nutritious alternative.

As your parent gets older, their immune system becomes less effective, which means that their ability to fight off infections and viruses reduces. It also means that it will take longer to recover from illnesses that are relatively common and that conditions such as flu and pneumonia can develop and even be fatal.

OSTEOPOROSIS

Osteoporosis is the common condition of thin, brittle bones. It is a serious condition that is often diagnosed only after a fracture has occurred. In the UK, one in two women and one in five men over the age of 50 will break a bone mainly due to osteoporosis. More women die from the after-effects of osteoporotic fractures than from all female-related cancers.

As with other parts of the body, bones grow and strengthen during childhood and peak in the mid-20s. From then on, the body constantly repairs and renews the bone but becomes less effective from around the age of 40. As a result, everyone has a risk of developing osteoporosis, but other factors can increase the chance. For women, a lack of oestrogen, perhaps caused by early menopause or hysterectomy increases their chance of developing osteoporosis. For men, low levels of testosterone can have the same effect.

If a close relative suffers from osteoporosis, the chance of developing the condition is increased. Also, various illnesses and medical treatments as well as heavy drinking or smoking can enhance its likelihood.

If your parent has broken a bone after a minor bump or fall they may already have osteoporosis and should discuss this with their GP.

Diagnosis of osteoporosis

Osteoporosis is usually diagnosed from a bone scan after a fracture. People do not tend to notice things until they start to go wrong. With osteoporosis, that can be when the bone has already thinned to the point of fracturing or breaking easily.

However, it can be diagnosed before a bone fracture by means of a bone density scan. Although in some areas of the UK these scans are not easily available, if your parent is at risk of osteoporosis it is worth discussing the possibility of a scan with their GP.

The test, called a dual-energy X-ray absorptiometry (DEXA) scan, measures the density of bones. It is currently the most accurate and reliable means of assessing the strength of bones and the risk of fracture. It is a simple, painless procedure that uses very low doses of radiation.

Treatment of osteoporosis

If your parent has osteoporosis or is likely to develop it there are treatments that can strengthen existing bones. The kind of treatment your parent has will depend on a number of factors including age, sex, medical history and which bones are broken. Supplements of calcium and vitamin D can be of benefit for older people in reducing the risk of osteoporosis.

For more information visit the National Osteoporosis Society website (see chapter 6).

PARKINSON'S DISEASE

Parkinson's disease is a progressive condition that hits the brain and central nervous system, affecting muscle control, movement and balance. It is caused by the loss of specialised nerve cells and their connections within certain areas of the brain.

The risk of developing Parkinson's increases with age, and symptoms often appear after the age of 50. Some people may not be diagnosed until they are in their 70s or 80s.

Is Parkinson's hereditary?

Although there is no conclusive proof that Parkinson's is hereditary, there does seem to be a genetic susceptibility to the disease.

People with siblings or parents who developed Parkinson's at a younger age have a higher risk of developing it themselves. This suggests it could be passed on in some families if, for example, they both come into contact with other factors such as a certain kind of food, or a particular chemical or virus. In such cases environmental and lifestyle factors will interact with the genetic susceptibility to trigger the development of Parkinson's.

Relatives of people who were older when they developed the disease have the same average risk for Parkinson's as the rest of the population.

Symptoms of Parkinson's

Symptoms can involve movement and behaviour. It is a very individual type of illness, but for 70 per cent of people the first symptom in movement is a tremor, which usually begins in one hand. As the condition develops, there can be a slowing down of movement and stiffness in the muscles which can make actions such as standing up or rolling over in bed difficult. Other common symptoms include sleep disturbance, constipation, urinary urgency and depression.

All of these, however, may have other causes than Parkinson's and there are no special tests that can prove whether or not someone has it. It is not an easy disease to confirm and diagnosis is usually made on a person's medical history and medical examination.

Treatment for Parkinson's

As there is no cure for Parkinson's, it is the symptoms that are treated. If the symptoms are not too severe, the first priority might be simply to follow a good exercise and diet regime. When problems get worse, symptoms are treated with a variety of drugs and specialist care from speech and occupational therapists. Sometimes, surgery may be considered appropriate.

For more information visit the Parkinson's Disease Society website (see chapter 6).

PERIPHERAL ARTERIAL DISEASE (PAD)

Peripheral arterial disease (PAD) is a narrowing of one or more arteries (blood vessels). It mainly affects arteries that take blood to the legs. The condition is also known as 'peripheral vascular disease' and may be referred to as 'hardening of the arteries'. People with PAD have a higher-than-average risk of having a stroke or heart attack.

In the UK, at least 1 in 20 people over the age of 55 have some degree of PAD. It becomes more common with increasing age. The typical symptom is pain which develops in one or both calves when walking. This pain is due to narrowing of the femoral artery, which is the most common site for PAD to develop. When you walk, the calf muscles need an extra blood and oxygen supply. The narrowed artery cannot deliver the extra blood, and so pain occurs from the oxygen-starved muscles. The pain soon goes when you slow down or stop. The pain comes on more rapidly when you walk up a hill or stairs than when you walk on the flat.

As with many diseases, there are a number of self-help measures that people who have it can take. They should:

- stop smoking
- exercise regularly – walking is the best form of exercise and should be done daily. Patients are advised to walk until the pain develops and then rest for a few minutes before starting again, aiming to walk for at least 30 minutes. The pain is not damaging to the muscles. Research studies show that if a patient stops smoking and exercises regularly symptoms of PAD are unlikely to become worse, and they often improve. The risk of developing heart disease or a stroke will also be reduced
- eat a healthy diet
- take care of the feet: injury may lead to an ulcer or infection developing more easily if the blood supply to the feet is reduced.

The self-help measures above are the most important part of

treatment. In addition, medication is often advised. Surgery is needed in only a small number of cases.

Medical treatments include taking a daily low dose of aspirin, which does not help with symptoms of PAD but helps prevent blood clots (thrombosis) forming in the arteries and reduces the risk of heart attack or stroke.

Most people with PAD do not need surgery. Your parent's GP may refer them to a surgeon if symptoms of PAD become severe, particularly if they have pain when resting. Surgery is considered a last resort; it is not easy, or without possible complications. Treatment includes:

- angioplasty, in which a tiny 'balloon' is inserted into the artery and 'blown up' at the narrowed section. This widens the affected segment of artery but is only suitable if a short segment of artery is narrowed
- bypass surgery, in which a graft (like a flexible pipe) is connected to the artery above and below a narrowed section. The blood is then diverted around the narrowed section
- amputation of a foot or lower leg. This is needed in a small number of cases when severe PAD develops and a foot becomes gangrenous due to a very poor blood supply.

For further information, contact the British Heart Foundation (see chapter 6).

PNEUMONIA

Pneumonia is an infection which affects the spaces and airways in our lungs. It usually affects children or people over 65 and is more likely to develop after another illness such as flu.

Pneumonia symptoms

The main symptoms of pneumonia are similar to flu. The person will feel feverish, with aches and pains and a poor appetite, and will also have a cough. This may be a dry cough at first, but will then produce phlegm. Depending on which part of the lung is affected they may also have a sharp pain in their side.

If you are concerned about your parent's health and think they may have pneumonia you should arrange an appointment with the doctor.

Pneumonia treatment

If bacteria cause the pneumonia it can usually be easily treated with antibiotics. Viruses do not respond to antibiotics, but if the pneumonia is caused by a virus, antibiotics may be used to help prevent any secondary infections.

If the pneumonia is severe, or the person is either very old or frail, they may need to be treated in hospital where antibiotics and extra fluids and can be given straight into the vein (intravenously). If breathing is difficult, extra oxygen can be given through a face mask. About one in every six people with pneumonia are ill enough to need this kind of specialised care.

Recovering from pneumonia

People recovering from pneumonia are advised to rest and drink plenty of fluids. If they over-exert themselves when ill, they can prevent their immune system fighting off the illness.

Over-the-counter medicines can be used to reduce fever, body aches and cough. Most people make a full recovery, although feelings of tiredness can linger for some time. Pneumonia can be severe and it is as well to be aware that some people may die of this condition.

Precautions against pneumonia

The first precaution for anyone over 65 or with a weakened immune system, heart or lung condition is to have a flu jab in the autumn.

Also, if your parent smokes, encourage them to stop as smoking increases the chances of developing pneumonia.

PRESSURE SORES

Pressure sores are areas of damaged skin and tissue that develop when sustained pressure — usually from a bed or wheelchair — cuts off circulation to vulnerable parts of the body, especially the skin on buttocks, hips and heels. Without adequate blood flow, the affected tissue dies.

Although people living with paralysis are especially at risk, anyone who is bedridden, uses a wheelchair or is unable to change position without help can develop bedsores.

Bedsores can develop quickly, progress rapidly and are often difficult to heal, particularly in older people whose skin is already thin and papery.

Initially, a pressure sore appears as a persistent area of red skin that may itch or hurt and feel warm, spongy or firm to the touch. In people with dark skin, the mark may appear to have a blue or purple cast.

If the pressure is not relieved, the skin may rub off and the wound becomes an open sore that looks much like a graze. At the same time, it is possible that the lower levels of skin that have also been deprived of circulating blood will also have been damaged. If the sore has not been recognised as such, the damage will extend down and a crater-like wound will be created.

If left untreated, eventually a large-scale loss of skin occurs, along with damage to muscle, bone, and even supporting structures such as tendons and joints. By this stage, the pressure sore will be difficult to treat, slow to heal and can cause serious complications of infection.

People who use a wheelchair are most likely to develop a pressure sore on:

- the base of the spine and buttocks
- the shoulder blades and spine
- the backs of arms and legs where they rest against the chair.

For people who are bed-bound, pressure sores can occur in any of these areas:

- the back or sides of the head
- the rims of ears
- shoulders or shoulder blades

- hip bones and lower back
- the backs or sides of knees, heels, ankles and toes.

Prevention and treatment of bed sores
If your parent suffers from limited mobility and sits for long periods or cannot easily turn over in bed, their carer needs to regularly check their body for the tell-tale redness that can indicate the beginning of a pressure sore. It should be massaged to encourage the blood circulation and vigilance maintained to ensure that the area is relieved from pressure.

As soon as there is any skin damage, your parent's doctor should be informed and a visit arranged for the district nurse. Treatment at an early stage will be with ointments and dressings. If the sore is further developed, it will probably be necessary to have daily visits from the nurse, who will use specialised dressings and treatments.

PROSTATE PROBLEMS
As men get older, changes in the prostate, which is part of the male reproductive system, can lead to serious health problems.

Knowing what symptoms to look out for or how to be tested to check whether there is a problem could literally, in the case of prostate cancer, save a man's life.

The prostate is a gland, normally the size of a walnut, located close to the base of the bladder in front of the rectum. It produces fluids that nourish and protect sperm and which are an important ingredient in semen.

The prostate gland is wrapped around the urethra, which is the tube that carries urine out of the bladder. Because of its location it is difficult to examine the prostate directly without a rectal examination.

All men's prostate glands get bigger as they get older. This is the cause of the condition known as benign prostatic hyperplasia (BPH).

Prostatitis
Prostatitis is inflammation of the prostate gland. Although it sounds like a straightforward condition, there are many different types with

a variety of symptoms, and causing various levels of pain to men of any age.

Symptoms of prostatitis may include:

- pain or burning when urinating;
- lower back pain;
- pain on ejaculation;
- needing to urinate frequently – including at night;
- feeling a sudden, almost irresistible need to urinate;
- having a weak stream, particularly when starting or stopping urinating;
- fever and chills;
- pain in the pelvic area;
- problems with urinating.

Some forms of prostatitis can be treated with antibiotics. It is also advisable to rest and drink lots of fluids. Treatment of other forms is often limited to pain control.

Prostate cancer

If diagnosed at an early stage, prostate cancer can be successfully treated but symptoms can be vague, easily missed and similar to other prostate problems.

Having a small amount of cancer within your prostate is actually very common.

About one in three men over the age of 50 have some cancerous cells within their prostate, and most men over the age of 80 have a small area of cancer in their prostate. Most of these cancers grow very slowly and do not cause problems, but for a small number of men the cancer can grow more quickly and become a risk to health.

The symptoms of prostate cancer include:

- pain when urinating;
- needing to urinate frequently – including at night;
- feeling a sudden, almost irresistible, need to urinate;
- a hesitant start to urinating;

- having a weak stream, particularly when starting or stopping urinating;
- needing to strain to urinate;
- pain on ejaculation;
- lower back pain or stiffness in the pelvis; and
- blood in the urine.

In its early stage prostate cancer often does not produce any symptoms.

Prostate cancer is most common in Western countries and research suggests that our diet is partly to blame for this. There are also indications that genes play a role in the chances of developing the disease: a man whose father or brother has had prostate cancer is about twice as likely to develop the condition as a man who has had no close relatives with it.

Ethnic background can also be a factor: men from African-Caribbean backgrounds are more likely to develop prostate cancer, while for those from Asian backgrounds it less likely.

Prostate screening

There is no organised screening programme for prostate cancer, but if your father is concerned about the health of his prostate, he can ask his doctor for a prostate-specific antigen (PSA) test. The PSA is a blood test that can give an indication of whether prostate cancer is likely to be present. However, the doctor may also recommend a digital rectal examination to assess the health of the prostate.

For more information, visit the Prostate Cancer Charity's website (see chapter 6).

RHEUMATIC DISEASES

Osteoarthritis affects around 8.5 million people in the UK. It is a disease of the joints which mostly affects the knees, hips, feet and fingers. Most people who have it are over 65 and women are more likely to have osteoarthritis than men.

As we get older cartilage can become brittle and rough. The bone beneath the cartilage tries to compensate and ends up creating knob-bly growths known as osteophytes or 'bone spurs'. The synovial membrane can get thicker, which reduces the space inside the joint and can lead to inflammation. Cartilage can break away from the bone leaving the ends of the bones to rub together. This is very painful and can lead to the joint changing shape.

Osteoarthritis does not develop according to a set pattern. Changes can be very gradual. Most people find that their joints become stiff and painful to move.

Exercising regularly and carefully to maintain strong muscles and flexible joints should help delay the onset of osteoarthritis. Joints do not 'wear out' with use: it is lack of use that puts them at risk. Obese people are six times more likely to develop the disease than those at their ideal weight, so a healthy diet is also important.

If your parent has developed osteoarthritis, exercises can be very helpful – but they need to be the correct exercises: seek professional advice from a physiotherapist.

Inflammatory arthritis is caused by swelling and tenderness inside the tough layer of tissue that forms a protective capsule around the joint. The synovial membrane usually helps to lubricate the joint, but when it becomes inflamed it can stop the joint from working well. This inflammation can also damage the cartilage and bone. It is impor-tant to try to treat the inflammation at an early stage.

The most common type of inflammatory arthritis is **rheumatoid arthritis**, caused by the body's normal defence system going into action against the soft tissue within joints. It is not clear why this reaction happens. Rheumatoid arthritis can affect people at any age, but it most commonly develops between the ages of 30 and 50. Women are three times more likely to develop it than men.

For four out of five people with rheumatoid arthritis the condi-tion develops slowly over several months. For other people it can develop very rapidly. The inflammation tends to go in cycles and the amount of damage that is caused to the joints varies from person to person.

Again, early treatment is essential in order to try to prevent long-term damage.

Soft tissue rheumatism is a general term to describe pain that is caused by damage to the ligaments and tendons of a joint rather than the bone and cartilage. This can lead to pain in a specific place, such as the elbow ('tennis elbow'), or it can be a more general pain.

'Housemaid's knee' is a particular type of soft tissue rheumatism caused by bursitis, the condition that also causes bunions.

Bursitis is an inflammation of the fibrous tissue that lubricates tendons where they pass over bones. It usually affects the knee, but can occur in any joint including the toes (bunions) and elbow. The best way to prevent bursitis is to avoid long-term pressure and rubbing on joints when possible. Make sure that shoes fit properly, and use knee pads when doing gardening or housework.

Treating rheumatic diseases

Exercise is essential for keeping joints supple, strong and mobile, and needs to be done even if the joints are affected by osteoarthritis. In general, people with arthritis should aim to exercise every day, although there may be days when joints are particularly stiff and inflamed and it might be necessary to rest more than usual.

Exercise should always be taken steadily. Seek advice from the doctor or physiotherapist.

Hydrotherapy, which may be available at a local swimming pool, can help with muscle-strengthening.

Medication Three main types of medication are available for arthritis:

- pain-relieving medicines (analgesics)
- anti-inflammatory medicines
- disease-modifying medicines.

Although analgesics are available over the counter from a chemist, before using them to treat arthritis it is a good idea for your parent to discuss them with their doctor. Anti-inflammatory medicines are prescribed if there is inflammation as well as pain in joints, as reducing the inflammation may help reduce the damage to the joints. Disease-modifying medicines affect the immune system and are used for rheumatoid arthritis. They can have severe side-effects and are usually prescribed by a hospital specialist such as a rheumatologist.

Complementary therapies such as osteopathy and acupuncture have been shown in studies to relieve the pain of arthritis. It is vital to find a trained and reputable practitioner. Search the British Complementary Medicine Association website (see chapter 6) for a practitioner in your area.

Dietary supplements of fish oils and glucosamine sulphate have been shown to offer benefits to people suffering from arthritis. The fatty acids that are found in fish oil and some plant seeds may help to relieve inflammation in the joints, which should help people with rheumatoid and osteoarthritis. However, research is still ongoing. Healthy eating guidelines recommend that we eat fish twice a week and one of these helpings should be oily fish, such as salmon, mackerel or sardines.

Hot and cold packs Pain and stiffness can be relieved by warmth. There are creams that produce a localised heat, but a hot-water bottle, or a heat pack warmed in a microwave, would also be worth trying. Make sure that the source of heat has a fabric cover so that it does not burn the user.

If joints are hot and inflamed an ice pack might help to calm them down. It is advisable to check out with your parent's physiotherapist or doctor whether ice will help the condition and, again, make sure the pack has a cover as ice can burn if it is directly applied to the skin.

For more information visit the websites of the charities Arthritis Care and Arthritis Research Campaign (see chapter 6).

STROKE

About 150,000 people suffer from a stroke each year in the UK, and most of them are over 65. Most will need care following the stroke. Although its impact varies widely from individual to individual, stroke is a major cause of disability and the fourth most prevalent cause of death in the UK after cancer, heart disease and respiratory disorders.

Men are more at risk from stroke than women and nearly one person in every three who has a stroke will die within the first year following the stroke, usually in the first ten days. Of those who survive, about 65 per cent will make a reasonable recovery, but 35 per cent will still need a great deal of help to manage with day-to-day tasks, often from both family and professionals.

Strokes occur when the blood supply to part of the brain is disrupted and brain cells are deprived of the oxygen and nutrients they need. As a result, an area of brain tissue may become damaged or die. Strokes are disabling in many ways: they can cause physical disability, are the cause of about 20 per cent of all types of dementia and frequently result in depression.

There are two main types of stroke: ischaemic and haemorrhagic. The first occurs when a blood clot blocks one of the arteries carrying blood to the brain. The second is the result of a rupture of a blood vessel and bleeding in or around the brain.

Mini-strokes

Mini-strokes, sometimes referred to as 'transient ischaemic attacks' (TIA), occur when the blood supply to the brain is briefly interrupted. The symptoms are very similar to stroke but they last for less than 24 hours and there is always complete recovery. However, people who experience a mini-stroke are at much higher risk of stroke and should see their GP immediately to see what preventative measures they can take.

The effects of stroke

The effects of stroke vary from person to person. They will depend upon where the stroke took place in the brain and whether it was mild or severe, as well as on the individual's age and general health.

Common physical symptoms of stroke include numbness, weakness or paralysis affecting one side of the body, or just an arm, leg or one side of the face. There may also be difficulties in communicating

RECOGNISING A STROKE

The sooner someone is diagnosed and treated after experiencing a stroke, the better the outcome. The Face Arm Speech Test (FAST) is a form of stroke identification which can be used by non-medical people to assess the three neurological signs of stroke:

1 Ask the person to SMILE.
2 Ask them to RAISE BOTH ARMS.
3 Ask them to SPEAK A SIMPLE SENTENCE (coherently), such as 'It is sunny out today'.

If the person has trouble with any of these tasks, call 999 and ask for an ambulance.

due to slurring or loss of speech or problems in understanding what is being said. Some people may experience difficulties in swallowing, incontinence, unsteadiness or disturbed vision.

Other symptoms that can be equally disconcerting and upsetting for everyone include loss of concentration, tiredness, memory problems and depression. In the blink of an eye, a previously healthy person can be rendered incapable of looking after themselves or even holding a conversation. It is a devastating condition to experience or witness.

In some cases, symptoms may lessen or disappear over time; in others they may remain.

Treatments for stroke

Despite the fact that much can be done to prevent stroke, treatment options for the condition are few. It is usually simply a matter of trying to assist recovery through good nursing and therapeutic care.

Your parent may be prescribed drugs (possibly aspirin) to prevent a further stroke and to treat any other underlying conditions such as high blood pressure and cholesterol. Even people with normal levels of cholesterol, suffering from either heart disease or stroke, may be given cholesterol-lowering drugs as part of their treatment.

Reducing the risk of stroke

There is no single underlying cause of stroke. Risk factors can include existing medical conditions such as high blood pressure, high levels of cholesterol, diabetes, heart disease and thickening of the arteries (arteriosclerosis).

Lifestyle changes that can help to reduce the risk of stroke and improve general health include:

- giving up smoking
- drinking alcohol only in moderation
- doing regular physical exercise
- keeping weight at a sensible level
- eating a healthy diet, low in fat, salt and sugar and high in fruit and vegetables
- having blood pressure checked at least once a year.

For more information about stroke visit the Stroke Association website (see chapter 6).

VISION

Macular degeneration

The most common cause of poor sight for those over 65 is age-related macular degeneration (AMD), whereby the central part of the retina, used for seeing colour and fine detail, deteriorates.

AMD is an age-related process that can develop after the age of 50. The exact cause remains unknown, and there is currently no effective treatment for most cases of AMD.

AMD is not painful and almost never leads to total loss of sight, although it is the most common cause of registered blindness for older people in the UK. The degeneration of the macula can leave a central blind spot which makes it difficult to read, watch television and recognise faces. However, the side (or peripheral) vision of those with

AMD remains intact and, with practice, can be enough for people to maintain an independent life.

Glaucoma

In an opposite way to AMD, glaucoma initially affects peripheral vision. In this condition, because there is damage to the optic nerve at the back of the eye, abnormally high pressure builds up, which causes loss of vision. If not promptly treated, glaucoma can lead to 'tunnel vision', where only objects directly in front of the person can be seen, and ultimately to blindness.

Glaucoma usually develops after middle age and the chance of having it increases as we get older. There are different forms, and like so many diseases it tends to run in families; different genes, however, run in different families. As well as being more prevalent in people from specific ethnic groups – for example, people from African-Caribbean backgrounds are four times more likely to develop glaucoma than those from European backgrounds – it can also develop at a younger age in those groups. It is also more common among people who have diabetes or illnesses that require the use of oral or inhaled steroids.

Treatment can be very successful if started early. It may be eye drops or, if necessary, surgery.

Cataract

Another common problem for older people is cataract, in either or both eyes. A cataract is a clouding of the eye's natural lens which lies behind the iris and the pupil. Like a camera lens, it adjusts the eye's focus.

To begin with, a cataract starts out small and at first has little effect on sight: there will be simply a little blurred area towards the centre of vision. Gradually, however, all of the vision becomes blurred, and it will be like looking through a cloudy piece of glass. It may also make light from the sun or a lamp appear too bright and glaring.

If your parent develops a cataract, stronger reading glasses or bifocals will help them see more clearly in the early stages, but eventually they will need a simple operation to remove the cloudy lens and replace it with an artificial one.

More information on all these conditions can be found on the RNIB website (see chapter 6).

GOING INTO HOSPITAL

'I have been admitted about three times over the last 20 years and have always had problems with the food. I'm Type-2 diabetic and the hospital diet breaks all the rules of healthy eating.' *(father)*

'We really do appreciate the NHS and currently benefit from many of its services and facilities. These are all on offer (or for the asking).' *(father)*

'When I needed surgery they asked me to choose a hospital, but I did not know where treatment might be better so I opted for the nearest place.' *(father)*

If your parent is taken to hospital either for routine treatment or in an emergency, it can be an anxious time for you both. If your parent relies on state benefits to maintain a reasonable standard of living, these may be affected, and worrying about money can add to the strain for you both.

BENEFITS AND HOSPITAL STAYS: THE 28-DAY RULE

Hospital stays that are 28 days or less apart are added together and counted as one stay when calculating how long your parent has spent in hospital. For all benefits, including Attendance Allowance and Disability Living Allowance, the day on which your parent is admitted and the day on which they leave hospital are not included in the 28 days.

It can be tricky to work out exactly how benefits will be affected by a stay in hospital. If your parent is worried, call the Help the Aged SeniorLine service (see chapter 6).

ATTENDANCE ALLOWANCE AND DISABILITY LIVING ALLOWANCE

Attendance Allowance and Disability Living Allowance (care component) are suspended after 28 days in hospital. The mobility component of Disability Living Allowance will continue to be paid while your parent is in hospital if they have a Motability agreement. Any balance which would have been paid will stop after 28 days. If your parent does not have a Motability agreement, the mobility component may be cut to the lower rate after 28 days in hospital. (See 'Keeping mobile' on page 134).

If your parent gets one of these benefits and is going into hospital they must inform the Disability Living Allowance and Attendance Allowance helpline (or, for Northern Ireland, Disability and Carers Service, part of the DWP) straight away (see numbers in chapter 6).

Remember to inform the helpline when you know that your parent is going to be discharged from hospital or is discharged so that the benefits can be reinstated.

CARER'S ALLOWANCE

If you are claiming Carer's Allowance for your parent, you may be able to continue to receive Carer's Allowance for up to 12 weeks out of a 26-week period; this will depend on how long you have been their carer and whether you have had a break within the last 26 weeks. If your parent loses their disability benefit when they are in hospital, your Carer's Allowance will stop at the same time. If your parent is a carer and goes into hospital, their Carer's Allowance will stop after 12 weeks; this may be sooner if they have been in hospital or had a break within the last 26 weeks.

If your parent has to go into respite care, your Carer's Allowance will stop after four weeks, unless an arrangement pattern of respite care can be made that allows them to keep their Attendance Allowance or Disability Living Allowance. In this case, you would be able to continue to receive the Carers Allowance. For more information on this, call the Carer's Allowance Unit (or the Disability and Carers

Service if you are in Northern Ireland): see chapter 6 for contact details.

PENSION CREDIT, COUNCIL TAX BENEFIT AND HOUSING BENEFIT

Pension Credit can sometimes continue to be paid indefinitely without being reduced or stopped when someone goes into hospital. It is divided into two parts – guarantee credit and savings credit. Your parent can get either or both of these, and they are affected in different ways by a stay in hospital. Generally, Council Tax Benefit and Housing Benefit will not be lost or reduced until your parent has been in hospital for 52 weeks, unless there has been a change in their pension credit.

If you have any questions about your parent's Pension Credit, Council Tax Benefit and Housing Benefit during a hospital stay, call the Help the Aged SeniorLine service (see chapter 6).

STATE RETIREMENT PENSION

Your parent's State Retirement Pension will be paid in full for the whole time they are in hospital, no matter how long the stay. Previously, State Retirement Pension was 'downrated' after a hospital stay of more than 52 weeks. This rule was abolished in April 2006.

OTHER BENEFITS

Some other benefits are paid in full during a stay in hospital. These benefits are:

- Incapacity Benefit
- Severe Disablement Allowance
- Bereavement Allowance
- Widowed Mother's Allowance/Widowed Parent's Allowance
- Widow's Pension
- Industrial Death Benefit
- Unemployment Supplement.

War Disablement Pension can often be increased during a stay in hospital, if the treatment is for the war injury. For more information call the Veterans Agency (see chapter 6).

HELP WITH THE COST OF TRAVELLING TO HOSPITAL

If your parent's income is low, they may be able to get help with the cost of travelling to hospital. If your parent is entitled to help, payment is made at the hospital when they visit. The hospital receptionist who deals with fares will need to see proof of entitlement, such as a Pension Credit award letter or an HC2 or HC3 certificate.

Your parent can get certificates HC2 and HC3 if their income is low but they do not qualify for the guarantee credit part of Pension Credit. To apply, your parent should fill in form HC1, which they can get from the NHS hospital or by calling the Department of Health (see chapter 6). They may also be able to pick one up from the local benefits office or doctor's surgery.

PATIENTS' RIGHTS IN HOSPITAL

All patients have a legal right to a reasonable standard of care and treatment from hospital staff. What is defined as reasonable is judged by what other members of the same profession would do in similar circumstances.

There are also some basic standards which NHS hospitals are required to meet. These include:

- respect for privacy, dignity and religious and cultural beliefs;
- respect for confidentiality;
- a clean and safe hospital environment; and
- a named nurse in charge of your care, and name badges to be worn by all staff.

If you have any worries about the standard of care your parent receives in hospital, try to raise your concerns directly with the staff involved, or the nurse in charge of the ward. If this does not help, you can make a formal complaint (see 'Making a complaint', page 22).

PATIENTS' RIGHT TO INFORMATION

Your parent has the right to have any proposed treatment, including the risks and any alternatives, clearly explained before they agree to it. Doctors should reply fully and truthfully to any questions patients ask about their health and treatment. However, doctors can withhold information if they think this is in someone's best interest, although this does not happen very often.

If your parent feels that they are not being told enough, it is more likely to be through a lack of communication rather than any deliberate attempt to keep them in the dark. Talk to the doctor about your parent's concerns, and make sure you ask for them to have an explanation of anything they are unsure about.

Your parent has a right to see their medical records, although they do not have the automatic right to see written records that were made before November 1991.

YOUR RIGHTS TO INFORMATION ABOUT YOUR PARENT

If your parent is perceived by the hospital staff as competent and makes clear to them that they do not want you or other family members to be informed about their health, that is their right. Only if the medical professionals think that observing the confidentiality of your parent would put either their health or that of someone else at risk may they disclose any information if they have specifically been asked not to. Most likely, though, your parent will be anxious that you are as informed about their condition as they are.

Nevertheless, when you visit your parent in hospital and perhaps make an appointment to speak to their doctor, always include your parent if at all possible. After all, it is your parent's health, well-being and quality of life that are being discussed and it is their decisions that should take precedence, not yours. But if your parent's illness has made them confused or unable to communicate effectively, it is advisable to have previously discussed with them their preferences with regard to medical intervention.

As suggested earlier in this guide, as your parent gets older, it is worthwhile to have in place an enduring power of attorney or a lasting power of attorney set up in case your parent becomes unable to look after their own affairs effectively. With regard to medical decisions, however, the LPA is far more effective as it gives you the right to make decisions about your parent's health and personal welfare if they become unable to make rational decisions.

PATIENTS' RIGHT TO REFUSE TREATMENT

Anyone is normally free to refuse any treatment or medication as long as they understand what this refusal will mean. A doctor can only examine and treat someone without their consent in certain circumstances: for example, if they are:

- unconscious and cannot indicate their wishes;
- detained under the Mental Health Act; or
- temporarily incapable of giving consent: for example, due to drugs or alcohol.

If someone is forced into having any treatment they do not want, this can be treated as an assault.

If you have a lasting power of attorney for your parent, it will be your decision whether or not your parent should receive a course of medical treatment. If your parent is very ill, this can be a very difficult decision to make.

COMING OUT OF HOSPITAL

'My mother had a stroke and went straight into the home afterwards.' (*daughter*)

'Before she came home, the hospital made sure that she could manage the stairs but we were always worried about her after that fall.' (*son*)

Coming out of hospital can be a time of mixed feelings for you and your parent. Although you will be pleased that your parent is well enough to return home, both you and they may have some worries about how they will cope. These worries should be addressed before your parent is discharged from hospital.

HOSPITAL DISCHARGE

The process of leaving hospital once a patient is well enough is called hospital discharge. Your parent's consultant will decide when they are medically fit enough to be discharged, but the final decision might involve several different people: perhaps the nurses on the ward, the GP and staff from the local council social services department (England/Wales), social work department (Scotland) or health and social services trust (Northern Ireland).

The decision that your parent is to be discharged should not come as a surprise: planning for the time when they leave hospital should begin almost as soon as they are admitted. You should ask to be kept informed throughout your parent's hospital stay of everything that is being done to plan for their discharge.

Every hospital has a hospital discharge procedure. This is intended to make sure that every patient who leaves hospital has the support and help they need. One member of staff, usually a nurse, will be responsible for co-ordinating the arrangements and making sure everything is in place before your parent is discharged. Discharge arrangements can vary a lot, depending on particular needs and on whether your parent is returning home from hospital or going into a care home.

HOSPITAL DISCHARGE FOR PEOPLE GOING HOME

The arrangements that are made will depend on your parent's needs. They may just need some basic help – perhaps advice on medication and a letter to their GP. Or they may need help with practical matters such as arranging transport and preparing their home for their return. Some people need a good deal of support and assistance to help them manage at home.

HELP FOR PEOPLE WHO NEED SUBSTANTIAL SUPPORT

If you or the hospital think your parent will continue to need care once they get home, you can ask the local council to assess their needs (see 'Care assessment', page 18). This is so that they can decide what sort of services your parent will need. Local council social services departments (England/Wales), social work departments (Scotland) and health and social services trusts (Northern Ireland) are responsible for arranging services to help older and disabled people to stay in their own homes. The services that the local council might provide include:

- **home help** – assistance with general household tasks
- **home care** – help with personal care, such as washing and dressing
- **meals on wheels**
- **day care** – perhaps a place at a local day centre
- **respite care** – residential care, or care provided in your parent's own home, to give you a break if you have become their carer
- **aids and adaptations** – to make living at home easier to manage.

The case study overleaf looks at how Mrs Smith is helped to return home from hospital despite having no family living nearby. It should give you an idea of how arrangements might work out for your parent.

HELP FOR PEOPLE WITH FEWER CARE NEEDS

Not everyone needs this sort of detailed assessment of their needs. Some people go home from hospital fully able to carry on with everyday life, while others have family, friends or neighbours who can help out for a while until things settle down. None the less, one member of the hospital staff will still be responsible for making sure that everything is in order before your parent is discharged, whatever their care needs may be. Even if you are able to arrange most things to help your parent yourself, this staff member can still provide help and advice.

MRS SMITH LEAVES HOSPITAL

Mrs Smith lives alone and recently fell over, fracturing her hip. She has been in hospital for some time but is now walking with the help of a frame and is keen to get home. Her son, who lives a hundred miles away, is worried about how she will manage. He discusses his concerns with the hospital staff, who arrange for a Care Assessment before Mrs Smith is due to be discharged. The local council care manager, occupational therapist, physiotherapist, hospital consultant and GP talk to each other, and to Mrs Smith with her son present, about the help she will need to manage at home.

It is agreed that Mrs Smith will have a daily visit from a home care worker for the first few weeks of her return home. The occupational therapist arranges the supply of a bath seat and a commode. The physiotherapist gives Mrs Smith advice on improving her walking and sets up some physiotherapy appointments.

As Mrs Smith lives alone and would like more company, the care manager arranges a place at a day centre for two days each week. Mrs Smith does not go home until everything is arranged. She settles in well, and after a few weeks her needs are reassessed. She is now walking well, and does not need daily home care visits, so these are reduced to two each week. However, Mrs Smith continues to go to the day centre and knows that she or her son can contact her care manager if she needs more support in the future.

This member of staff will also be responsible for making arrangements on your parent's behalf if you cannot make them. Even if your parent does not need a full community care assessment, they may still have some contact with staff from social services, or with an occupational therapist, physiotherapist or dietician. They might also have some contact with the community nursing service if they will need visits from the district nurse.

It is important to talk to whoever is in charge of your parent's discharge if you or they are not happy with any of the arrangements being made. Be sure to explain exactly what your concerns are, as they may be easily addressed. But if you feel that your parent is not going to manage, do say so. It might be better for your parent's care needs to be fully assessed by the social services department. You are entitled to ask for this sort of assessment if you feel your parent needs it.

GOING HOME FROM HOSPITAL

Even if your parent has had a community care assessment and has a care plan sorted out, there are still practicalities to consider, particularly if you are not available to go home with your parent on discharge. Do they have clothes to go home in? Will there be food in the house? If the weather is cold, will the house be warm?

You should be told the date and time of your parent's discharge in advance, so that if you cannot be there you have enough time to prepare for their return home. The following sections give an idea of the sort of things you need to think about.

Remember that the hospital has a responsibility to check that everything is in order before your parent goes home, and to ensure arrangements are made for them if you or they have not been able to make them yourselves.

TRANSPORT

How will your parent get home? If you cannot offer a lift or ask for another relative or friend to do it, perhaps you can arrange for a taxi or minicab. Some hospitals have volunteer drivers who can take people home, or occasionally the nurses on the ward may arrange for someone to be taken home by ambulance.

It is up to the member of staff responsible for your parent's discharge to make sure that suitable arrangements are made; so talk to him or her if you are aware of any problems.

If your parent receives the guarantee credit part of Pension Credit, or they are on a low income, they may be able to get some help with the cost of transport home. Ask the member of staff responsible for your parent's discharge about this. Your parent can claim for public transport fares, petrol costs if travel is by private car, or contributions towards a local voluntary transport scheme. Taxi fares will be paid only if there is no other way your parent can travel for all or part of the journey.

CLOTHES, KEYS AND CASH

Does your parent have clothes to go home in, including shoes and a coat? You may need to take into the hospital whatever is needed. Check that they have their front-door key and enough cash for things like taxi fares.

PREPARING YOUR PARENT'S HOME

The house needs to be ready for your parent's return. If they went into hospital unexpectedly, it may have been left in a mess. If you cannot go in to tidy up, maybe you know of friends or neighbours who might be willing to do so.

If you live far away and there is no one you can ask to help you, talk to the hospital staff member in charge of your parent's discharge arrangements; perhaps a home help or volunteer could go to the house and get it ready for your parent. Sometimes voluntary groups like the Red Cross, WRVS and Home from Hospital offer services to help people who are being discharged; ask hospital staff if there is a scheme like this running in your parent's home locality.

Other things that need to be done in the home include switching the heating on, making up your parent's bed, getting in basic food supplies and preparing a meal for their return.

If your parent needs a piece of special equipment, such as a bath seat or a walking frame, this should be supplied before they are discharged. They will also need to have been trained in how to use it. In the same way, if the home needs to be adapted in some way, these adaptations should be made before your parent goes home.

CHECKING THAT SERVICES ARE READY TO START

If your parent is going to receive services such as a home help or meals on wheels, check with the hospital that these will begin as soon as your parent is discharged. If they were receiving this sort of service before going into hospital, the social services department needs to be told that they are coming home and that services should resume. Hospital staff should also get in touch with the community nursing team if your parent needs visits from the district nurse.

CHECKING THAT BENEFITS ARE IN ORDER

Most benefits are not affected by a stay in hospital. However, Attendance Allowance and Disability Living Allowance are stopped after four weeks in hospital. Carer's Allowance is stopped after 12 weeks (and in some cases before). If your parent's benefits have been affected by the stay in hospital, tell the benefits office that your parent is home as soon as they are discharged. This will usually mean that the benefits can be restored to their previous level

MEDICINES AND HEALTH ADVICE

Your parent may be given some medicine to take home. Make sure that you and they know what each medicine is for, and how often they need to take it. This information is important, so ask for it to be written down and keep a copy for yourself if you think this would be helpful. It is also a good idea to check that your parent can open the medicine or pill bottles: 'child-proof' lids can sometimes be adult-proof as well. Your parent will probably be given supplies to last for a week or two, so make sure they know how long they should carry on taking each of the medicines supplied. Your parent may need to get a repeat prescription from their GP.

Your parent might also be given information and advice about diet and exercise. Make sure that they understand what they have to do; do not be afraid to ask for more explanation if necessary, or for information to be written down for future reference. There is often a great deal for people to take in when they are discharged from hospital and your parent may feel overwhelmed.

MEDICAL FOLLOW-UP

Your parent may be asked to come back to the hospital for a follow-up appointment, or for regular check-ups. They should be given full details of these appointments before they leave the ward. Or they may be told to make an appointment to see their GP. If possible, make sure that you too know what medical follow-up is made. You can then check that the various appointments are made and kept. **It is very important that your parent keeps these appointments even if they are feeling completely well again.**

You also need to know what to do should you or your parent have any problems or worrying symptoms following discharge. If this is not mentioned, ask the member of staff taking care of the discharge arrangements.

Finally, the consultant and medical team will contact your parent's GP with details of your parent's discharge date, diagnosis, treatment and medication. The GP will also be told about the arrangements that have been made for their care. This information should be sent to the GP within 24 hours of your parent leaving hospital.

IF YOUR PARENT CANNOT GO HOME YET

If it looks like your parent is going to go on needing a good deal of care and support, it might be suggested that moving house could make it easier for them to cope – perhaps a move into sheltered housing, or to a smaller, more manageable house, would be the best solution. But for some people the result of the community care assessment may be different. After discussion with medical and nursing staff, one of the following options might be suggested.

CONTINUING NHS HEALTH CARE (ENGLAND, SCOTLAND AND WALES)

It could be decided that your parent needs to stay in hospital, or needs care provided by the NHS in another setting such as a nursing home, hospice, their own home or even yours. There will probably be quite complex medical reasons behind this decision, often to do with the type or intensity of your parent's healthcare needs and a requirement for regular supervision from NHS staff. Every Strategic Health Authority (England), NHS Board (Scotland), Local Health Board (Wales) or Health and Social Services Board (Northern Ireland: these will become Strategic Health and Social Services Authorities from 1 April 2008) has its own set of rules – known as eligibility criteria – for deciding exactly who can get this type of care. Ask the hospital for a written explanation of these rules. If it is decided that your parent does need this sort of continuing NHS health care it will be arranged and paid for by the NHS.

EXTRA TIME FOR RECOVERY

Your parent should on no account return home until they are really able to manage. The hospital does not want to have to admit them again because things did not work out when they got home. So in some situations it could be decided that they need either more time to recover fully or a spell of rehabilitation: that is, extra help and attention to help them get back to normal. The Strategic Health Authority (or national equivalent: see above) will have rules for working out whether your parent is entitled to this kind of care.

If your parent is assessed as needing a period of rehabilitation or recovery, it will be arranged and paid for by the NHS. In some parts of the country they may be offered intermediate care – a type of 'rehabilitation and recovery' service which is intended to help people recover their independence and get back to living at home.

Intermediate care is fairly short-term – it will not last longer than six weeks – and it may be provided in a hospital, a care home, or the person's own home. If the NHS provides your parent's intermediate care it will be paid for by the NHS.

CARE IN A CARE HOME

After your parent's Care Assessment, it may be suggested that they will not be able to manage at home, even with a lot of help and support from social services. However, their consultant may say that they are medically fit enough to be discharged and that they no longer need hospital care.

Your parent may therefore be offered the option of moving into a care home, although for some time it has been government policy to encourage older people to stay in their own homes (or those of their relatives).

Moving into a care home is a big decision. You and your parent will need time to think it over – it is not something to be rushed into. Your parent should be involved at all the different stages of their assessment and be assured that their feelings are paramount in any decision about where they should live. There could be other possibilities: for example, maybe they could manage at home if they had extra support, or perhaps a move into sheltered housing would be the answer. (See chapter 2.)

DISCHARGE FROM HOSPITAL INTO A CARE HOME

It could be, however, that moving into a care home is right for your parent.

In the final instance, this has to be your parent's decision, not yours. It is natural for them and you to have some reservations, but if they feel reasonably happy with the idea, moving into a care home can be a positive step. Although it can be difficult coming to terms with the idea of not going back home, they may feel more secure and comfortable living somewhere that can meet their needs. They may also feel that they will be less of a burden on you and other members of the family if professional carers have the responsibility of looking after them.

However, it is important that they know that they are loved and that they will still be an integral part of family life even if they live in a care home.

PROBLEMS WITH DISCHARGE INTO A CARE HOME

You may be happy with the idea of your parent moving into a care home, particularly if you have worries about how they would manage at home. However, you need to be aware that **no one can be discharged into a care home against their will**. This could be because they think they could manage at home: if this is how they feel, you need to talk to them with the person who carried out their assessment for community care services, because your parent's wishes should *always* be taken into account during an assessment; maybe other services could be offered that would help them cope at home.

However, it may be that they do not wish to be discharged into a care home as they feel they still need the sort of care that can only be provided by the NHS. As mentioned above, each Strategic Health Authority (England), NHS Board (Scotland), Local Health Board (Wales) or Health and Social Services Board (Northern Ireland – soon to become Strategic Health and Social Services Authorities) has its own rules (or 'eligibility criteria') for working out if someone is entitled to carry on getting care under the NHS. But if your parent has *not* been assessed as needing this sort of continuing care, they do not have the right to stay put in a hospital bed indefinitely. The social services/social work department of the local council has a responsibility to work with hospital and community-based staff, and with your parent and yourself, to try to find another acceptable way of meeting their needs. But if you cannot reach agreement the hospital can discharge your parent to their home. Care services must be arranged for them at home before they can be discharged in this way. However, these services might not cover all of their needs as government guidance says that such services only have to be provided 'within the options and resources available'. Your parent may also have to pay for the care services provided by the social services/social work department.

Being discharged in this way can be distressing for everyone involved. So as a final check before your parent is discharged, they (or you or another member of the family or carer) have the right to ask for a review. This review will look at the decision that has been made about your parent's entitlement to continuing NHS in-patient care. Usually the Strategic Health Authority (or national equivalent: see above) will seek advice from an independent panel. This panel will have an independent chairman, and will include a representative of the health authority or board and the local council.

The panel has to consider whether the rules for deciding whether your parent needs continuing NHS care have been correctly applied. It is not able to look at whether the rules themselves are fair. Members of the panel will speak to you and your parent, and may also get advice from hospital staff. The panel can also ask for independent clinical advice on your parent's condition if they think this would help. The panel's recommendation does not have legal force, but it is expected that the health authority or board will usually accept its view.

In January 2006 a significant case (the Grogan case) highlighted the fact that some health authorities are using over-restrictive criteria to decide whether individuals are entitled to free NHS care. Strategic Health Authorities and their national equivalents have been told to review their eligibility criteria in order to ensure they are being applied correctly.

If you feel that your parent should be entitled to NHS-funded continuing care, but that the eligibility criteria are unreasonable, ask the primary care trust to review their care needs again in the light of these events.

For more advice on this issue contact the Help the Aged Senior-Line service.

ELDER ABUSE

'I grit my teeth sometimes to stop me shouting at her.
I know it's not her fault, but she can't seem to stop
twittering.' (*daughter*)

'They said it was because her skin was so delicate, but I
made it clear that I wasn't pleased to see the bruising on
her arms.' (*son*)

It is widely accepted that young children who are unable to look after
themselves are sometimes abused, either by their own family or by
carers. Until the 1990s, older people were rarely considered to be
vulnerable in the same way, and yet the *UK Study of Abuse and Neglect*,
published by the National Centre for Social Research in June 2007,
states that just under 5 per cent of the over-60s have suffered
unkindness or worse in the past year. Given that abuse is frequently
at the hands of family members and loved ones, it is thought that the
true figure may be much higher. Also, the study only covered older
people living in the community: abuse in care homes could be harder
to expose.

Abuse comes in different forms:

- physical abuse (the most obvious form): being hit, slapped or kicked;
- neglect: not being adequately fed, clothed or given medication;
- bullying: may include being threatened, humiliated or verbally abused.
- theft: this could mean taking items without permission, or using your parent's money, including pension or benefits, without authorisation;
- sexual abuse: could mean being inappropriately touched when being helped to dress or bathe, or worse.

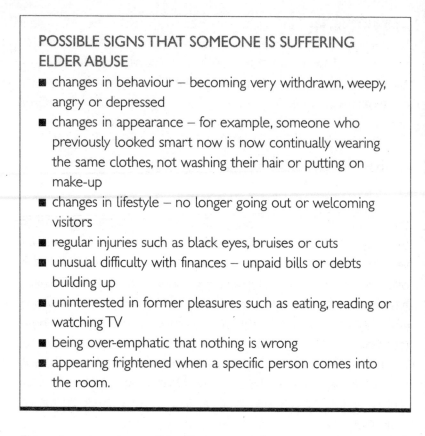

POSSIBLE SIGNS THAT SOMEONE IS SUFFERING ELDER ABUSE

- changes in behaviour – becoming very withdrawn, weepy, angry or depressed
- changes in appearance – for example, someone who previously looked smart now is now continually wearing the same clothes, not washing their hair or putting on make-up
- changes in lifestyle – no longer going out or welcoming visitors
- regular injuries such as black eyes, bruises or cuts
- unusual difficulty with finances – unpaid bills or debts building up
- uninterested in former pleasures such as eating, reading or watching TV
- being over-emphatic that nothing is wrong
- appearing frightened when a specific person comes into the room.

Elder abuse is not something that can only happen to someone else's parent. We could all be guilty of elder abuse, even if unintentionally. It can happen when rushing your parent to finish their meal or hurrying them into their coat. By being in a hurry, you could handle your parent roughly and bruise them. Also, the stress of constantly having to look after someone should not be underestimated. Although unacceptable, it is understandable that sometimes you could get angry with your parent for their slowness at using the toilet or washing their hands. It is especially exasperating to care for someone who suffers from dementia and is forgetful and confused. You could easily end up shouting at them and subsequently feel guilty, knowing that they were doing their best.

If you think losing your temper with your parent could become a problem for you, it is particularly necessary for you to get regular breaks from caring. Speak to the social worker or doctor to see what day centre amenities are available or if some additional outside care can be arranged. If you do not address the issue, your parent will wonder what they have done to deserve your anger, they will be confused and worried that if they mentioned it, you would no longer be willing to look after them.

If your parent lives in residential care or another family member is their primary carer, it can be awkward if you suspect abuse. Even if your parent is sometimes confused, do not ignore any comments they make with regard to cruelty. Rather than exaggerate any mistreatment, they are more likely to be reluctant to complain and will very often cover up any violence they have experienced. They will offer convincing, innocent explanations about how a bruise or swelling has appeared. But even if they do not tell you something is wrong, you may notice a change in your parent that rings alarm bells (see box).

If you are worried that your parent is being mistreated, you may be concerned about being 'interfering' or 'getting it wrong' and therefore decide not to say anything. But it is important that you try to help; your parent is vulnerable.

- Talk to your parent about your worries.
- Give them the opportunity to respond. Make it clear you want to listen.
- Whatever they have to say, stay calm.
- If they ask you not to tell anyone, do not make false promises. Always be honest.
- Ask your parent what they would like to happen. It may have taken them a long time to get the courage to tell you what has been going on, so do not expect an immediate answer.

Action on Elder Abuse (see chapter 6) assists people who need advice, information and support on this issue. ■

COMING TO
THE END

'My father was with her all of the time and I was pleased. They were so much in love that it was right that he should be the one with her then.' (*daughter*)

'The staff at the hospice were wonderful. Thoughtful, considerate – we couldn't have asked for more.' (*son*)

There are many different ways to prepare for the end of someone's life, but in the case of a parent you should if possible take time with them to consider what they want. You will also need to be able to deal with their emotions and your own, and to consider the other members of your family and your parent's close friends.

PREPARING FOR THE END OF LIFE

Before your parent's health becomes too poor, you should encourage them to make a will if they have not already done so and to put in place a lasting power of attorney or living will (see pages 121 and 124).

Even if your family has a strong religious faith, dying itself remains the great unknown experience and if your parent knows they are dying they are likely to experience strong emotions. Just thinking about death will remind them of others they have loved and lost during their life. It may make them aware of unfulfilled ambitions and angry about what they will miss. Their anger may be misdirected at you or other family members; it could simply be a symptom of feeling helpless, worthless and impotent. Some people become very spiritual as they approach death whereas others who may have always had a powerful religious faith during their life may experience doubts and question any existence of an Almighty.

Although logically you may know that you have always done your best for your parent, you too may also feel helpless and guilty that you are unable to help them now. Death awaits us all but it is natu-ral to have fear of the unknown. All you can do is reassure your parent that you are there for them and that you love them.

END-OF-LIFE CARE

If your parent is diagnosed with a serious illness such as advanced can-cer for which the only treatment is aggressive chemotherapy or radiotherapy, or radical surgery, they may prefer to opt for 'palliative care'.

The aim of palliative care is to prevent and relieve pain and suf-fering and to improve the quality of life for people facing serious, complex illness. This may be a difficult decision for you to accept, but the alternative, though perhaps offering a slightly longer life for your parent, is one which involves difficult and painful medical treatments. It is hoped that you will have discussed your parent's wishes with regard to aggressive medical treatment before they become this ill and that you will have come to terms with any decisions they have made.

If they have chosen palliative care, this may be given in a hospice rather than a hospital. Hospices are smaller and more personal than hospitals and the staff are specialised in caring for the dying and their families.

If your parent has suddenly been taken ill, or is not able to recover following surgery, their death may take place in hospital; well over half the population dies in hospital. If they have had a long terminal illness, your parent may have already spent some time in a local hospice which could be their preferred place to die. Alternatively, they may prefer to end their life in the privacy of their home. Wherever possi-ble, let the choice of where they die be their own.

If you are worried about coping with a death at home, discuss the help you can expect to get with your parent's doctor. Are there specialist nurses (for example, if your parent has cancer, a Macmillan or Marie Curie nurse) who might be able to make frequent visits, or could a local hospice offer hospice-at-home services?

THE FINAL HOURS

One of the first signs that the end of life is near is that activity decreases, with less movement, less communication and less interest in the surroundings. This apparent lack of interest is part of the natural process of withdrawing from the world and should never be interpreted as a snub to you or any other loved one. Attempting to eat, drink and swallow becomes difficult and you may need to coax your parent to take a sip of water. Eventually, the time comes when food and drink are neither wanted nor needed. The use of a mouth swab and applying a salve to the lips can help to relieve a dry mouth.

Towards the end various changes will take place in your parent's body. Their temperature and blood pressure will fall, and circulation will diminish, making the hands and feet feel cool compared to the rest of the body; their skin colour will become duller and their fingernail beds will turn bluish rather than their normal pink or brown.

Occasionally, in the last hours of life, a noisy rattle develops in the breathing due to the build-up of mucus in the chest that can no longer be coughed up. Although you may find this distressing, the sound is not an indication of pain or suffering. The dying person will speak less, then not at all. Coma, which may last for minutes or hours before death occurs, often follows. Since people in comas can sense and hear others around them, you should remember this and continue to talk to and touch them. Sing softly to them or read a poem that you know they like; it will help them feel less alone and less afraid.

For most people, the final moments of life are very peaceful, with their breathing becoming gradually slower and more irregular before stopping. Death is indicated when the chest no longer rises and there is no breath from the nose. Your parent's eyes may be glassy and no pulse will be felt. This is a very still, quiet moment and you will probably feel bereft. You will have lost one of your parents, someone who has had a pivotal role in your life, who has been around for good or ill since the moment you were born.

If your parent's health has been deteriorating over a long period of time, you will already have been grieving for the person they once were. But death is the final loss from which there can be no return.

At such times it can help to have other family members close by who can help you through this desperately sad time.

PRACTICAL ARRANGEMENTS FOLLOWING A DEATH

'The lady at the registry office was very helpful and explained everything that needed to be done.' (*son*)

'Although there's a lot to be done, once I'd got probate, the official stuff was straightforward. What was awful was sorting through the house – we'd all grown up there and it was like throwing away all that our parents had worked so hard for.' (*daughter*)

Most deaths need to be registered within five days, in the area where the death occurred. In Scotland you have eight days in which to register a death.

When you get the medical certificate you should be given the address of the local registry office: if not, ask. Many offices now see people by appointment only, so it is advisable to phone ahead and arrange a convenient time to go in. You or another relative needs to take the certificate to the registry office. You will also need to take birth and medical certificates, medical card, pension and benefits books. The registrar needs this information to complete the formalities. You will then be given these documents:

- certificate of burial or cremation, to be given to the funeral director;
- certificate of registration of death;
- extra copies of the death certificate if you need them: it is advisable to have a few extra copies for dealing with the will and other business. You usually have to pay for these copies.

POSTMORTEMS

A postmortem is a medical examination of the body. Postmortems are usually carried out where there is uncertainty about the cause of death.

Postmortems can be requested by the coroner (an independent official who inquires into unnatural death – for example, sudden, unexpected or those related to procedures or operations) – or by the hospital or close relatives; permission of the close relatives of the deceased must be sought if the hospital wants a postmortem to be carried out but no permission is needed if the postmortem is requested by the coroner.

Postmortems usually take place within a couple of days of the death and the body is released on the day of the postmortem, so planning for the funeral should not be affected. Following the postmortem, reports are sent to the GP/consultant of the deceased and the coroner (if applicable), relatives can also request a copy.

For more information about postmortems contact NHS Direct (see chapter 6). You can also find out more on the government's website, www.direct.gov.uk/death.

ARRANGING A FUNERAL

You do not have to hold a funeral or cremation immediately, unless you want to or it is the standard practice of your parent's religion. It may be helpful to wait a little while to ensure the arrangements are exactly what you want, and to give some notice to the people who want to be there. However, you should contact the funeral director as soon as possible. Funeral directors can help you make the arrangements and advise you on all the official forms and procedures. They will collect your parent's body from the hospital or from your home, and keep it until the funeral.

If your parent did not hold religious beliefs, there is no reason for the funeral to have a religious theme. It is becoming increasingly popular for families to arrange for friends and family members to speak at funerals. Equally, religious songs can be replaced by music that you and your family feel is more representative of your parent and appropriate

PAYING FOR A FUNERAL

Find out how you are going to pay for the funeral before you go ahead with the arrangements. Often the bank or building society will be prepared to release money to pay funeral costs from the account of the person who has died, even before probate (see below) has been granted. The cheque might be made out directly to the funeral director. You need to check the following:

- did your parent have a prepayment funeral plan whereby they paid for the funeral in advance of their death?
- did your parent have a pension scheme or insurance plan which included a lump sum for funeral costs?
- if your parent had money in National Savings, could a lump sum be released?
- did your parent belong to a union or professional association which pays benefit when a member dies?

You yourself may also be able to get help towards the cost of a funeral if you are in receipt of certain benefits such as Working Tax Credit. You can ask for further information on this when you register your parent's death.

to your family's values. Although funerals are public ceremonies to mark the end of a life, which is a sad time for the family and friends, they do not have to be wholly sombre affairs, but can be a celebration of the deceased person's life. You may wish mourners to remember your parent with flowers or, if you have discussed it with your parent before their death, you may prefer donations to a charity of your parent's choice.

Funeral costs

Funeral costs can be paid out of your parent's estate (their money, property and possessions). However, it may be some time before that money is available and the funeral director may need payment before then.

You should get quotes from at least two funeral directors and make sure that you know what the quotes include. Coffins vary enormously in price, and you also need to know what the charges are for the hearse, any other cars and the pall-bearers. Even quite simple funerals can cost a good deal of money.

PROBATE

It is hoped your parent will have left a will specifying what they want done with their estate. If there is a will, it will specify who your parent wanted as executor to carry out their wishes. If you are the executor, in order to get access to your parent's assets you will need to get a grant of probate from the Probate Registry to give you the authority to do so. If your parent left no will but had money or property, an application for legal authority to administer the estate should be made to the Probate Registry. The Probate and Inheritance Tax Helpline (see chapter 6) can give you details of your local registry, and can also give you general advice on getting probate. In Northern Ireland contact the Probate Office.

GRIEF AND MOVING ON

'Years ago, after my grandmother died, I remember my dad telling me that when a parent dies you feel guilty about all the things that you should have done for them but didn't. Then you have to stop and remind yourself that you did your best. And I did.' (son)

'I miss my mum every day and still cry easily when I think about her. I know I'm lucky to have a loving husband and family, but no one can replace what she meant to me.' (daughter)

The first time you experience the death of a parent you will have feelings that you have probably never felt before. They may be so overwhelming and strong that you weep uncontrollably and feel physically ill; you may even believe that you will no longer be able to continue with everyday life. You will see strangers going about their daily lives and feel as if you are in a different universe. On the other hand, you may feel numb or even guilty for not feeling as sad as you think you should. Everyone's reaction is different. There is no right or wrong when it comes to dealing with grief.

In addition to your own grief, you may be left with a widowed parent who has no wish to carry on living without their partner. Unlike some societies, the UK is one where older people are encouraged to live independently after the death of a spouse or partner. As a result, older people, who may have married young, are suddenly and for the first time in their lives expected to live alone. Their utter loneliness and sadness can affect you greatly when you are trying to come to terms with your own loss.

If your parent had a painful terminal illness, at the same time as feeling sad about their death you may also feel relieved that their suffering has come to an end. Your feelings may be mixed up and contradictory and sometimes difficult to admit to. Perhaps your relationship with your parent was difficult, and now that they have died you are finding the time to consider their life and your part in it.

However you feel, you can only live through the event in your own way.

TALKING ABOUT YOUR PARENT

You may want to talk about your parent with friends and family; this is a common way to remember them and to grieve for them. However, your friends may be reluctant to mention your parent in conversation, fearing that you could be upset. If necessary, tell them that you want to talk and share memories about your parent, remembering the good times as well as the sad.

EMOTIONAL TURMOIL

Immediately after the death, you are likely to feel shock even if your parent was ill and you knew that they were dying. The reality of the death will still hit you hard and you may feel physically ill from its force. After a while, the immediate shock will wear off but you may still feel waves of sadness overwhelm you intermittently, where you cry uncontrollably and wonder if you will ever come to terms with the situation you find yourself in. More than likely, there will be times when you automatically do something as if your parent were still alive. This can happen whether you were involved daily with your parent before their death or whether you lived far away and kept in touch mainly by phone. It is very common and does wear off in time.

Feeling sadness is normal, as is feeling a level of relief, especially if your parent lived through a long illness. It is important to allow yourself time to grieve, and if you were spending a lot of your time looking after your parent you need to think about your own life and future.

The funeral can be a key moment in helping you and other people who were close to mourn. It is a formal, public event when your parent's life can be thought of, valued and celebrated. It is a time to think of the whole of the person's life, and not just of the difficulties of the last few weeks, months or years when they had perhaps become more difficult and dependent on others.

FEELING GUILTY

If you have been used to being your parent's primary carer, you are likely to be weighed down by the conflicting emotions of guilt and freedom, grief and happiness. Although you may have loved your parent dearly and looked after them well, you are now free to live your own life and perhaps spend more time with, say, your partner and, if you have them, your children. Many aspects of caring can make people feel guilty, and now that the caring is over you may feel guilty about being pleased that the tremendous responsibility involved has been cast aside.

All these feelings are common with carers. The main thing to remember is that you did what you could do. Having your own life is your right, and not something that you should feel guilty about enjoying.

At the same time, you may be apprehensive about the future. If in recent years you have been bound up daily with the care of your parent, you may feel frightened about what you are going to do with your life now.

MOVING ON

Losing a parent is a major event in anyone's life, but if you have been looking after your parent on a daily basis their death will bring enormous changes to your circumstances. If you have been sharing your home or theirs, it will feel empty after their departure. In addition, their death may cause a drop in the household income that could be a cause of concern. Alternatively, you may see it as the chance for you to return to your own career, or start a new one.

No matter what, you will need time to come to terms with the death and its implications for you and your family. This may be the time to sort out your parent's estate and home. Sooner or later, you will have to go through their clothes and personal belongings and dispose of them. This will be another emotive situation that can prove painful but needs to be worked through. If at times life seems too difficult to cope with, there are organisations you can turn to such as Cruse Bereavement Care (see chapter 6).

Eventually, you will get used to not having your parent around and it will become your normality. Losing a parent is painful but the normal course of nature's path. Whatever relationship you had with your parent, you must recognise that it was a two-way affair and that you did your best.

Your parent's existence is not lost or forgotten while you are still alive and, in the same way, if you have children yourself it will continue through their descendants. Life goes on and even if right now you cannot ever imagine feeling joyful again, you almost certainly will one day. ■

SOURCES OF
FURTHER
INFORMATION

HELP THE AGED

207–221 Pentonville Road
London N1 9UZ
Tel: 020 7278 1114
Fax: 020 7278 1116
Email: info@helptheaged.org.uk
Website: www.helptheaged.org.uk
Help the Aged offers a wide range
of information, advice, financial and
practical services to older people,
some of which are listed below. The
Charity also carries out social and
biomedical research and campaigns
affecting older people's lives.

Care Fees Advice Service
Specialist advice for anyone entering
or already in care, regardless of
means.
Tel: 0500 76 74 76 (freephone)
Equity Release Service
Impartial advice on all aspects of
equity release. Tel: 0845 2300 820
Gifted Housing
A unique range of support services
and care benefits provided to people
who gift their home to the Charity.
Tel: 01225 447 800
HandyVan
A free home security and safety
service offered to older people who
meet charitable criteria.
Tel: 01255 473 999
Information
Information sheets and advice leaflets
on financial matters, health, housing,
home safety and much more can be
downloaded from the website, and
many are also available in print.
SeniorLine
Free, confidential and impartial advice
from trained advice workers on
benefits, care, health and community
services, and housing issues.
Freephone: 0808 800 6565
(Northern Ireland 0808 808 7575)
(Note that calls from some mobile
phones may not be free.)
Textphone: 0800 26 96 26
(9am– 4pm Mon–Fri)
SeniorLink
A home telephone response service
for immediate reassurance or
emergency assistance (24 hours).
Tel: 0845 053 2306
Wills Advice Service
Free, confidential advice on making a
will, for people of state retirement
age.
Tel: 020 7239 1965 for a free
information pack
Campaigns
Contact the Campaigns team if you
come across examples of age
discrimination:
campaigns@helptheaged.org.uk

OTHER ORGANISATIONS

Action on Elder Abuse
Astral House
1268 London Road
Norbury, London SW16 4ER
Tel: 0808 808 8141
Website: www.elderabuse.org.uk

Age Concern England
Astral House
1268 London Road
London SW16 4ER
Freephone information
0800 00 99 66 (8am–7pm)
Website: www.ace.org.uk

Provides useful advice and information for older people.

Alzheimer Scotland
22 Drumsheugh Gardens
Edinburgh EH3 7RN
Tel: 0131 243 1453
Fax: 0131 243 1450
Website: www.alzscot.org

Alzheimer's Society
Devon House
58 St Katharine's Way
London E1W 1JX
Helpline: 0845 300 0336
(weekdays, 8.30–6.30)
Website: www.alzheimers.org.uk
Alzheimer's Society and Alzheimer Scotland offer specialist advice for people with dementia, their carers and families.

Arthritis Care
18 Stephenson Way
London NW1 2HD
Tel: 0845 600 6868
Website: www.arthritiscare.co.uk

Arthritis Research Campaign
Copeman House
St Mary's Court
St Mary's Gate
Chesterfield
Derbyshire S41 7TD
Tel: 0870 850 5000
Website: www.arc.org.uk

Assist UK
Redbank House
4 St Chad's Street
Manchester M8 8QA
Tel: 0870 770 2866

Textphone: 0870 770 5813
Website: www.assist-uk.org
Assist UK leads a nationwide network of disabled living centres.

Benefits Enquiry Line
Tel: 0800 88 22 00
Textphone: 0800 24 33 55
Online disability benefit claims:
www.direct.gov.uk/disability

Benefits Now
Website: www.benefitsnow.org.uk
contains full information about Disability Living Allowance and Attendance Allowance and how to claim.

British Heart Foundation
14 Fitzhardinge Street
London W1H 6DH
Heart information line:
08450 70 80 70 (Mon, Tues, Fri
9am–5pm and Weds, Thurs
8am–6pm)
Website: www.bhf.org.uk

British Red Cross
44 Moorfields
London EC2Y 9AL
Tel: 0870 170 7000
Website: www.redcross.org.uk
Red Cross branches provide services that may include transport, home care and medical equipment loans (for example, wheelchairs). See phonebook for details of your local group.

Calibre Audio Library
Tel: 01296 432 339
Website: www.calibre.org.uk

Cancerbackup
3 Bath Place
Rivington Street
London EC2A 3JR
Tel. (freephone helpline):
0808 800 1234
Website: www.cancerbackup.org.uk

Care standards authorities
**Commission for Social
Care Inspection (England)**
33 Greycoat Street
London SW1P 2QF
Tel: 0845 015 0120
Website: www.csci.org.uk

**Care and Social Services
Inspectorate for Wales**
4–5 Charnwood Court
Heol Billingsley, Nantgarw
Cardiff CF15 7QZ
Tel: 01443 848450
Website:
www.csiw.wales.gov.uk/index.asp

**Scottish Commission for
the Regulation of Care**
Compass House, 11 Riverside
Drive
Dundee DD1 4NY
Tel: 0845 603 0890
Website:
www.carecommission.com

Carer's Allowance Unit
Tel: 01253 85 61 23
Textphone: 01772 89 94 89

Carers UK
20–25 Glasshouse Yard
London EC1A 4JT
Free carers' line: 0808 808 7777

(Weds, Thurs, 10am–12pm,
2pm–4pm)
Email: info@ukcarers.org
Website: www.carersuk.org

**Chest, Heart and Stroke
Scotland**
65 North Castle Street
Edinburgh EH2 3LT
Advice line: 0845 077 6000
Website: www.chss.org.uk
Specialist advice and guidance for
people who have had a stroke, their
carers and families. (See also Stroke
Association, below.)

Cinnamon Trust
10 Market Square
Hayle
Cornwall TR27 4HE
Tel: 01736 757 900
Website: www.cinnamon.org.uk
Specialist charity for older people
and their pets. Can help to re-home
a pet if its owner is unable to take it
to a care home.

Citizens Advice Bureau
Website: www.citizensadvice.org.uk
Free, confidential and independent
advice, face-to-face or by telephone.
See phonebook for local branch.

**Community Transport
Association**
Tel: 0870 774 3586

Companions2Travel
Website:www.companions2travel.com

The Continence Foundation
307 Hatton Square

16 Baldwins Gardens
London EC1N 7RJ
Helpline 020 7831 9831;
0845 345 0165
Website: www.continence-foundation.org.uk
Advice and information on
continence problems. See also
InContact, below.

Counsel and Care
Twyman House
16 Bonny Street
London NW1 9PG
Advice line: 0845 300 7585
(weekdays 10am–12.30pm,
2pm–4pm except Weds afternoons)
Email: advice@counselandcare.org.uk
Website: www.counselandcare.org.uk
Advice and information on finding a
care home and what to look for.

Crossroads Caring for Carers
Crossroads schemes help carers by
providing respite care attendants
while they have a break. A small
charge may be made for this service.
Contact the national office to find
out about schemes in your area.
Website: www.crossroadscare.co.uk

**Crossroads Caring for
Carers England and Wales**
10 Regent Place
Rugby CV21 2PN
Tel: 0845 450 0350
Website: www.crossroads.org.uk

**Crossroads Caring for
Carers Northern Ireland**
7 Regent Street
Newtownards

County Down BT23 4AB
Tel: 028 9181 4455
Website: www.crossroadscare.co.uk

**Crossroads Caring for
Carers Scotland**
24 George Square
Glasgow G2 1EG
Tel: 0141 226 3793
Website:
www.crossroads-scotland.co.uk

Cruse Bereavement Care
PO Box 800
Richmond
Surrey TW91RG
Tel. (helpline): 0844 477 9400
Website: www.cruse.org.uk
Promotes the well-being of bereaved
people, helping them to understand
their grief and cope with their loss. As
well as counselling and support it
offers information, advice, education
and training services.

DEMAND
The Old Chapel
Mallard Road
Abbots Langley
Hertfordshire WD5 0GQ
Tel: 01923 681 800
Website: www.demand.org.uk
DEMAND (Design and Manufacture
for Disability) offers advice on, and
manufactures, specialist disability aids.
See also Remap, below.

Department of Health
Tel: 0870 155 5455 for details of
health benefits and healthcare claim
forms, or help with the cost of
getting to hospital

Diabetes UK
Macleod House,
10 Parkway
London NW1 7AA
Tel: 020 7424 1000
Website: www.diabetes.org.uk

Disability Action
189 Airport Road West
Belfast
County Antrim BT3 9ED
Tel: 028 9029 7880
Website:
www.disabilityaction.org

**Disability and Carers Service
(Northern Ireland)**
Tel: 028 9090 6178 (Attendance
Allowance); 028 9090 6182
(Disability Living Allowance); 028
9090 6186 (carer's allowance)

Disability Equipment Register
4 Chatterton Road
Yate
Bristol BS37 4BJ
Tel: 01454 318 818
Website:
www.disabilityequipment.org.uk

**Disability Living Allowance and
Attendance Allowance helpline**
(England, Scotland or Wales)
Tel: 0845 7123 456
Disability Wales
Bridge House
Caerphilly Business Park
Van Road
Caerphilly CF83 3GW
Tel: 029 2088 7325 (use announcer
for Minicom)

Fax: 029 2088 8702
Website: www.disabilitywales.org

Disabled Living Foundation
380–384 Harrow Road
London W9 2HU
Helpline: 0845 130 9177
Textphone: 020 7432 8009
Website: www.dlf.org.uk

**Elderly Accommodation
Counsel**
3rd Floor, 89 Albert Embankment
London SW1 7TP
Advice line: 020 7820 1343
Website: www.housingcare.org.uk
Free advice to older people on
housing options. Comprehensive
database of care homes in the UK,
focusing on aspects directly related to
quality of life within the care home
setting.

Entitledto.co.uk
The website www.entitledto.co.uk
can be used to find out whether
someone is entitled to benefits.

Health Advice for Travellers
Tel: 0800 555 777 for free leaflet

Hearing Concern
95 Gray's Inn Road
London WC1X 8TX
Helpline (telephone and textphone):
0845 0744 600
Website: www.hearingconcern.org.uk

Help the Aged
Services for older people are listed
on page 214.

Home improvement agencies

England – Foundations:
01457 891 909
Wales – Care and Repair Cymru:
029 2057 6286
Scotland – Care and Repair Forum
Scotland: 0141 221 9879
Northern Ireland – Fold Housing
Association: 028 9042 8314

InContact

Satra Innovation Park
Rockingham Road
Kettering
Northants NN16 9JH
Te: 0870 770 3246
Website: www.incontact.org
Advice and information on continence
problems. See also Continence
Foundation, above.

Insulation and draught-proofing

Grants from local authorities:
England: 0800 316 2808
Wales: 0800 316 2815
Scotland: 0800 316 1653
Northern Ireland: 0800 181 667

Law Society of England and Wales

113 Chancery Lane
London WC2A 1PL
Tel: 020 7242 1222
Website: www.lawsociety.org.uk

Law Society of Northern Ireland

Law Society House
98 Victoria Street
Belfast BT1 3JZ
Tel: 028 90 231614
Website: www.lawsoc-ni.org

Law Society of Scotland

26 Drumsheugh Gardens
Edinburgh EH3 7YR
Tel: 0131 226 7411
Website: www.lawscot.org.uk

Macmillan CancerLine

Tel: 0808 808 2020 (Mon–Fri,
9am–10pm)
Email: cancerline@macmillan.org.uk
For information on cancer care and
Macmillan nurses.

Motability Operations

City Gate House
22 Southwark Bridge Road
London
SE1 9HB
Tel: 0845 456 4566 (enquiries about
purchase or lease of car)
Tel: 0845 607 6260 (enquiries to
route2mobility about purchase or
lease of wheelchair or scooter)
Website: www.motability.co.uk
Motability, a national charity, was set
up to assist disabled people with
their mobility needs. The Motability
scheme enables disabled people to
obtain a car, powered wheelchair or
scooter using government-funded
mobility allowances.
Motability wheelchair insurance plan:
tel. 01264 333030.

NAPA (National Association for the Providers of Activities for Older People)

Bondway Commercial Centre
Unit 5.12
71 Bondway
London SW8 1SQ
Tel: 020 7831 3320

Website: www.napa-activities.net
Information on arranging activities in
care homes.

National Osteoporosis Society
Camerton
Bath BA2 0PJ
Tel: 0845 130 3076
Website: www.nos.org.uk

NHS Direct
Tel: 0845 46 47

Parkinson's Disease Society
215 Vauxhall Bridge Road
London SW1V 1EJ
Helpline: 0808 800 0303
Website: www.parkinsons.org.uk
Specialist advice and guidance for
people with Parkinson's, their carers
and families.

Partially Sighted Society
7–9 Bennetthorpe
Doncaster
DN2 6AA
Tel: 0844 477 4966 (9.30am–4.30pm,
Mon–Fri)
Fax: 0844 477 4969
Website: see www.patient.co.uk

The Pensions Service
See phonebook for address of local
office.
Tel: 0845 60 60 265
Website: www.thepensionservice.gov.uk
Advice on pensions overseas:
0191 218 7777
Pension Credit claims: 0800 99 1234
(0808 100 6165 in Northern Ireland)
Help with making claims:
0845 60 60 265

Prescription Pricing Authority
Bridge House
152 Pilgrim Street
Newcastle Upon Tyne NE1 6SN
Helpline: 0845 610 1171
Patient services: 0845 850 1166
Website: www.ppa.org.uk

Princess Royal Trust for Carers
142 Minories
London EC3N 1LB
Tel: 020 7480 7788
Email: help@carers.org
Website: www.carers.org

**Probate and Inheritance Tax
Helpline**
Tel: 0845 30 20 900

**Probate Office
(Northern Ireland)**
Royal Courts of Justice
PO Box 410
Chichester Street
Belfast BT1 3JF
Tel: 028 9072 4678
Email: probate@courtsni.gov.uk

The Prostate Cancer Charity
First Floor, Cambridge House,
100 Cambridge Grove
London W6 0LE
Tel: 0800 074 8383
Website: www.prostate-cancer.org.uk

**Relatives and Residents
Association**
24 The Ivories
6–18 Northampton Street
London N1 2HY
Advice line: 020 7359 8136
Website: www.welres.org.uk

Supports care home residents and their relatives. Operates a helpline and has a network of local groups.

Remap
D9 Chaucer Business Park
Kemsing TN15 6YU
Tel: 0845 130 0456
Website: www.remap.org.uk
Advice on, and manufacture of, specialist disability aids. See also DEMAND, above.

Ricability
30 Angel Gate
City Road
London EC1V 2PT
Tel: 020 7427 2460
Website: www.ricability.org.uk
Ricability is the trading name of the Research Institute for Consumer Affairs (RICA), a national research charity dedicated to providing independent information of value to disabled and older consumers.

Royal National Institute for the Blind (RNIB)
105 Judd Street
London WC1H 9NE
Tel: 020 7388 1266
Helpline: 0845 766 9999
Website: www.rnib.org.uk

Royal National Institute for Deaf People (RNID)
19–23 Featherstone Street
London EC1Y 8SL
Helpline: 0808 808 0123 Textphone: 0808 808 9000
Tinnitus helpline: 0808 808 6666
Website: www.rnid.org.uk

RSVP (Retired and Senior Volunteer Programme)
Website: www.csv.rsvp.org.uk

SeniorLine
See Help the Aged (page 214).

Stroke Association
Stroke House
240 City Road
London EC1Y 8JJ
Tel: 0845 3033 100
Website: www.stroke.org.uk
(For Scotland, see Chest, Heart and Stroke Association, above.)

National Talking Newspapers and Magazines
Tel: 01435 866102
Website: www.tnauk.org.uk

Tourism for All UK
c/o Vitalise
Shap Road Industrial Estate
Shap Road
Kendal
Cumbria LA9 6NZ
Tel: 0845 124 9973
Fax: 01539 735567
Website: www.tourismforall.org.uk

Transport for London
Tel: 020 7222 5600

UK Home Care Association
Tel: 020 8288 1551

UK Identity and Passport Service
Tel: 0870 521 0410

Valuation and Lands Agency
Helpline: 0800 197 0611

Veterans Agency
(Treatment Group)
Norcross
Blackpool FY5 3WP
Tel: 0800 169 2277

Vitalise
12 City Forum
250 City Road
London EC1V 8AF
Tel: 0845 345 1970
Website: www.vitalise.org.uk
Provides holidays and respite care for severely physically disabled people, with or without their carers, at five purpose-built centres in the UK. Also offers special Alzheimer's holidays for people with dementia and their carers which are subsidised by the Alzheimer's Society.

Volunteer agencies
Volunteering England
Regents Wharf
8 All Saints Street
London N1 9RL
Tel: 0845 305 6979
Website: www.volunteering.org.uk

Northern Ireland Council for Voluntary Action
61 Duncairn Gardens
Belfast BT15 2GB
Tel: 028 9087 7777
Website: www.nicva.org

Volunteer Development Scotland
Stirling Enterprise Park
Stirling FK7 7RP
Tel: 01786 479593
Website: www.vds.org.uk

Wales Council for Voluntary Action
Baltic House
Mount Stuart Square
Cardiff CF10 5FH
Tel: 0870 607 1666
Website: www.wcva.org.uk

Wills Advice Service
See Help the Aged (page 214).

Winter Fuel Payments
Helpline: 08459 15 15 15

WRVS
Garden House
Milton Hill
Steventon
Abingdon OX13 6AD
Tel: 029 2073 9000
Website: www.wrvs.org.uk
The local WRVS (see phone book) may offer a choice of services including visiting schemes, shopping services, home-delivered meals, volunteer drivers and escort schemes in England, Scotland and Wales.

INDEX